Fred Smeijers **Type now**

a manifesto

plus **work so far**

Hyphen Press . London

Published by Hyphen Press, London, in 2003
on the occasion of the exhibition 'Fred Smeijers: work so far' at the Royal Academy of
Art, The Hague, as part of the second Gerrit Noordzij Prize

'Type now' and 'Work so far' text and illustrations copyright © Fred Smeijers 2003
'Glossary' text copyright © Robin Kinross 2003

Fred Smeijers's text was edited by Robin Kinross, London, who was also the editor of
the whole book. Françoise Berserik, The Hague, with Jan Willem Stas, Rotterdam,
designed the main text pages and oversaw production. This text was typeset and
made into pages by Jan Willem Stas in QuarkXPress; the typefaces section was set
and made into pages by Corina Cotorobai, Antwerp, and Ingo Offermanns, Antwerp,
in QuarkXPress. Corina Cotorobai designed the cover. The book was made and
printed in the Netherlands by Ando bv, The Hague

ISBN 0-907259-24-3

www.hyphenpress.co.uk

*All rights reserved: no part of this book may be reproduced in any form, by print,
photocopy, or any other means, without written permission from the publisher*

Contents

Introduction 6

Type now

    Traps of our present technology 10
    The commodity of type 14
    Artisan or designer 20
    Fifteen years of democratic type? 26
    The show goes on 44
    A new moral code? 51
        A code of conduct 56
        Glossary 60

Fred Smeijers: *work so far*

    Typefaces 67
        Commentary 98

    In colour 103
        Commentary 121

    Year by year 126

Acknowledgements 142

Introduction

Gerrit Noordzij once wrote:
> Form (the quality of shapes) and rhythm (the quality of the arrangement of shapes) are essential for all design. However, the designer will always have to consider many other aspects as well (fitness for purpose, colour, size, finish etc.). This complexity makes it difficult to study form and rhythm as such.
> It is necessary to concentrate on these two subjects.
> Letters are sheer form and writing is rhythm. This makes writing designate for the study of form and rhythm.*

I was a student when I first read these words and already much occupied with the writing and drawing of letters. As far as I can remember, I always had this interest; but it was only after becoming a student of graphic design at Arnhem that this interest became a serious one. And, most importantly, any writing or work with letters was encouraged as well as criticized by the typography teachers on the course. I owe a lot to Alexander Verberne, who was the most important teacher in stimulating and broadening my view of the world of letters. It was he who gave me a copy of Gerrit's booklet *The stroke of the pen*, in which these words form the opening sentences. This was in 1982, the year that book was published. Now, in our so-called digital world, and after twenty years — seventeen of which I have spent as a professional type designer, as well as a freelance teacher of 'letters' in several schools of art — these words have lost nothing of their value.

There have been many changes since 1982. In the world of type, every country has had its famous practitioners, each of them representing his or her country on the map of type design. The Netherlands is rather small compared, for example, with its neighbour Germany — one of the most important countries in the field of type. It was perhaps Germany that had the highest concentration of type designers in the early to mid twentieth century. Still, we had the luck to have people like Sjoerd de Roos and Jan van Krimpen, who succeeded in establishing an international reputation for themselves and for our country. After a gap, Dutch type design was continued by Gerard Unger, who really made his presence felt internationally with his Calvinistic designs. At that time, the mid-1970s to mid-1980s, Gerard was one of the younger type designers on the international scene. Type designers were rare animals, and education in the field was also rare, perhaps non-existent. Designs for text types were done by the establishment: within the industry or by people known to the industry. There were exceptions, but what happened outside the industry was mostly concentrated on making flashy designs for photocomposition and rub-down lettering (Letraset, Mecanorma) intended for display. The industry consisted of manufacturers of composing equipment. By the late-1980s it was an industry that was being turned upside down.

leesbaarheid staat in praktijk slechts gelijk met datgene waaraan men ge wend is maar dat wil niet zeggen dat indien we zouden kunnen wen nen aan iets dat leesbaarder is dan dat waaraan we thans gewend zijn geen poging zouden moeten doen het bestaande af te danken

Sample of a typeface I designed as a student at Arnhem, as reproduced in the Lecturis booklet *Letters in studie*.

In 1983, in ignorance of the days to come, the printer Lecturis in Eindhoven published a booklet in their documentary series, which showed some serious attempts at new type designs made by Dutch students.** This was just a glimpse of what was to come. The initiator and editor was Gerrit Noordzij, who by then was more than half way to creating a school of type designers. Noordzij managed to do this by making type design comprehensive. Students trained in his writing classes managed to get an eye for, and therefore could control, form and rhythm. This knowledge could be easily applied to letterforms, and so soon resulted in new designs for type. Over the years Noordzij improved his theories. His knowledge was put into practice in the first place by himself – and what better proof does a student need? Anyone willing to listen seriously to his words soon realized their power by visiting the bookshop around the corner. Gerrit was the house designer for the Amsterdam publisher Van Oorschot, where his typefaces could be seen in trial form on all the covers. Whether or not one liked Noordzij's work, it certainly stood for something. This was no humbug, but real basic design knowledge.

Another important stimulus was the creation of Mac-Ikarus. For me this software made all the difference in designing and producing fonts. Now theory, and all the skills that one could develop along with theory, could be put into real-time practice. It is probably no coincidence that the creator of Mac-Ikarus, Petr van Blokland, had been a student of Noordzij.

Gerrit has been responsible for the knowledge that may be consolidated in writing. Further, this knowledge has been put into practice, and transferred to others, by the old students of his who now have taken over his role at the Hague Royal Academy of Art. And now even some of their students have become active as teachers. So the Hague Academy is more important than it may seem at first glance, because it is quite likely that this is the only place in Europe where there is a profound tradition in type design education. What pleases me most is that it has a real presence. It is not slumbering, old-fashioned, or dependent on one or two almost-dead heroes. It is firmly rooted in tradition, yet alive and with enough connections to present-day practice (although there will always be plenty of room for more connections). A basic interest in form and rhythm alone is not the only reason why type design can be an interesting field for students of visual communication. The digital revolution is in many respects not more than a crisis, and a crisis demands change — new opportunities and challenges.

Another visionary who understood quickly about the digital possibilities was Erik Spiekermann. In 1988, together with some colleagues, he initiated FontShop, first in Berlin, then internationally. Although this is a commercial enterprise, with the making of money (not education) as a primary aim, it was Spiekermann who managed to lift it all up to an international level. Spiekermann had an eye for the quality of work being done in the Netherlands, and FontShop International was the instrument to spread it around the world. Directly and indirectly, there are many younger type designers who owe a lot to Erik. His interest in typography and type, combined with his own talents in these fields, made him an ambassador for Dutch type design and for new type in general. Spiekermann provided a mundane and open environment, in contrast to the world of the classical type designer, which is a very personal and closed one. Young designers, as well as students, could visit Berlin and work for him. He created real opportunities in which the kind of practical understanding that Gerrit taught could flourish.

As will be clear, the text of this book brings together some of my thoughts on type design today: its practice and how it is taught. It deals with matters that are still on the move — so, final conclusions are hard to make. Though some of the main features of the recent period are mentioned, this is in no way a systematic or chronological account of what has happened in the last fifteen years of type design and making. Instead, I try to give this phase of development a place in a broader perspective, and try to look what was good or bad about it.

* Gerrit Noordzij, *The stroke of the pen*, The Hague: Koninklijke Academie van Beeldende Kunsten, 1982, p. 5.
** *Letters in studie: letterontwerpen van studenten in het Nederlands Kunstonderwijs*, Eindhoven: Lecturis, 1983.

Traps of our present technology

Taking human nature as a starting point, we might claim very loosely that, indeed, not much changes over the years. The world created by humans does change, but human nature itself changes hardly at all. We are still the same jealous, greedy, vain, and in general not bad but very predictable and afraid minds that can be found back in the plays of Shakespeare and of writers in the ages before him. The same goes for our biological condition. The plague is still here, and without constant developments in biochemical science we are still vulnerable to it. Closer to home, we catch a cold every winter, and have done so for centuries. So the biological consistencies and laws which dictate the well-being of our bodies have not changed much. True, the guys showing their muscles on the cover of MAN magazine are probably healthier than a medieval citizen. But only because their technologically more developed environment lets them be so. But the David of Michelangelo is not badly built either. You can go further back. Apart from automobiles and electricity, Roman society had much in common with present-day Western civilization. ‖ So, over the ages everything around us seems to change, to some extent, except us. One of the most important and unchanged driving forces of human nature is the fact that we want to feel and to be comfortable. There are many ways to feel good, but the most important ones have a strict order. First: a full stomach; preferably with a guarantee that it can be filled again tomorrow, and the next day, and so on. The need to protect your body from the natural elements is second: protective clothing. Having reached this level, you need space where you can more or less do your thing: a home. You've got all that? Then you had better make deals with others who are in the same situation, to protect your mutual interests: an army to secure your area. Only with these conditions can your children have a safe haven, so they can start a normal life. Having reached that level, it becomes clear that such a life requires a lot of decisions, rules, and laws. You may be able to build a house twice as big as your neighbour's — if that makes you feel good — but keep your hands off his wife! ‖ After several ages of building dwellings and seducing people, it became clear to some of us that it is also possible to feel good simply by improving yourself. So having already found much satisfaction in wielding swords, shooting bows and arrows, and making castles, it finally became time to play a game of chess. Alas, not everybody was in the position to play chess. This was, for a very long time, the exclusive right of the rich and famous. But the fact remains that satisfying one's personal interests is probably an instinctive striving, embedded in every normal human mind, regardless of its intelligence or background. So only the time left over — from filling the stomach, clothing, having a house, a clear and simple set of rules in order to create a community — can be spent on personal interests. ‖ In order to create this leisure, the community to which you belong has to be an efficient one. Writing is an important factor in becoming efficient, and typography is a very efficient way of writing. Anything that deals with the improvement of the crucial processes needed to improve the community's efficiency in providing goods and services can be defined as technology. The consolidation, transfer and therefore the possible improvement of technology is important for a community. Writing, or better typography, plays a key role in this. So technology is essential in being a civilized human being: one who has access to leisure time. Institutions like the Museum für Druckkunst in Leipzig or the Enschedé Museum in Haarlem, or the St Bride Library and the new Type Museum, both in London, are from this point of view wise ventures. It is quite understandable that the people behind them should care about material which has little value from a business or economic point, but which once played a key role in our society. These collections never really get the support they deserve from the general public. We like to invest millions in a painting, but hardly care about the knowledge and equipment which has been so vital in bringing us this far. The fact that the Plantin-Moretus archives in Antwerp have now been put on the list of Unesco monuments is just a drop in the lake of the history of technology. ‖ Of course it is not just about technology. As well as the manuals and the technical articles, which are usually very vulnerable to the tooth of time — thanks to the role that they themselves play in the process of progress — there are also texts that are printed and published over and over again. These texts — classics of literature, philosophy and the human spirit — are important because they seem never to be outdated, providing food for thought for every generation. They usually act as a gauge for the degree of civilization within a certain community. All this is a very simplified picture, of course, but in the end I think it all comes down to this. ‖ Now, the more efficient a community is, the greater the chance of leisure time and the higher its degree of civilization. The West had its greatest set-back in the two world wars of the last century. Since then, apart from some fear during the Cold War years, this part of the world has been comparatively stable. There have been more than enough conflicts elsewhere, but (apart from the Balkans) we have seen no serious wars in Europe itself, the United States, and even Russia. So in the last fifty years technology has made huge leaps forwards, leading to the wizardly times of the present. For many fields, including type design, what is going on today is pure magic. Suppose in the early 1970s you said: 'Right, toss your pencils and gauges into the bin. In twenty years' time they will be useless. Then we will not need a single pencil to create a new typeface. It will even be possible to give somebody across the Atlantic a copy of the original that is a hundred per cent true. And, you know what, in order to do that we will not need copies, envelopes, stamps, or even an aeroplane. We will simply wire the original, because in fact there is no real original any more. And all this by means of a telephone connection and some satellites. And not just one typeface — no sir, our whole library can be there in just a few minutes, in real time.' If you had said this, the chances are that you would be put in the mad-house or at least cautioned for watching too much *Star Trek*. || Technological developments serve society. If we need better roofs, technicians work on better roofs. If we want to recycle waste material in a more efficient way, technologists will come up with some answers. If we want to have fun, bigger and better roller-coasters are built by the fun technical department. If we do not ask for anything quickly enough, technology will give answers anyway; for example, mobile telephones with built-in digital cameras, smaller than a Mars Bar. Even Agent 007 did not dream of this. Technology has become a force of its own and does not always serve mankind. In the first place it may serve itself. It is, after all, an industry, some parts of which seem to have no real questions to answer any more. So gadgets such as mobile phones with built-in cameras are really made, and people — usually kids — buy these precious items. And now you take a snapshot, wire it to your friend, and you can even call that friend to have some moments of shared joy concerning the event just caught. Cool? Fun? Yeah, cool and fun, you can't beat that. But what is actually happening here? Digital technology is being used to prove right away that you are having a good time, to prove right away that you are not a looser, that you actually have a life. Hey, look at this picture, you see me having fun here. See, I am alive! They make you believe that the picture is more important than the joyful event itself. The camera-phone sends only fun pictures, of course; it certainly does not send the bill. || The need to show that you had a good time is not new. Many of us remember the annual slide show of holiday pictures, taken somewhere in Italy. Nowadays we prefer to do this right away, as freshly as possible. Many things seem to get transformed into fast, short moments of joy. Any depth is then a hindrance. In these circumstances, where society embraces shallow but fast consumption, with experiences following one after another in rapid short cycles (and nothing seems to escape from this — ice creams, coffee, cars, even real estate), then it is no wonder that type design is reaching its highest peak ever.

The commodity of type

At the end of February 2003 in Heidelberg, Linotype held their second Typotechnica conference. It was a worthwhile and well-attended meeting, which did indeed highlight new technological developments within the world of type production. I stress the word production here, since design was not so much the issue; the main topic was all the technicalities of producing correct font files which work in the right, predictable way. All the large firms had sent representatives. They stressed that new fonts have to be technically sound. Now they even provide free programs, such as Microsoft's Font Validator, to check fonts before commercial release. And they are right to do so. Good designs are useless if they are not well produced; and fonts that cause trouble can be bad for business. Troublesome fonts can turn the computer into an irritating tool and will affect the reputation of all the parties involved. ‖ Clearly the conference, which dealt mainly with the new OpenType format, was held at the right time. We are at a turning point. The Western world is definitely digital now. There is a computer in every office and every household, and the rest of the world is following as fast as it can. Ordinary users, just as much as business people, believe that they have to communicate globally – have to be compatible with everybody, everywhere, all the time. ‖ This applies to images, music, and the bulk of the daily digital traffic: plain or even very complex text documents. Industrial standards provide the necessary fundament for developers, so that their software produces results that can be exchanged. So to do typography, we need standards – for the way in which language is encoded, and then for the way in which language is displayed in particular visual forms. ‖ The second area here is the one most apparent to any ordinary computer user: it is the domain of the font format. In the first phase of the 'PostScript revolution' the standard format was Adobe's PostScript Type 1. Then, in the early 1990s, TrueType was introduced by Apple,

now working in collaboration with Microsoft. This format showed significant advances over Type 1. But, at least in the Macintosh world, it was never really established as a new standard, for the usual reasons of muddle and imperfect implementation by particular companies and particular devices. There is a distinction to be made between commercial items that may or may not become 'de facto' standards; and standards that are developed to be standards from the outset, by cross-commercial committees and organizations, traditionally with offices in neutral Switzerland.
‖ The standards for encoding language in its written form have been of this second kind: they really are standards, not just systems that we accept because of the commercial weight behind them. The old standard for encoding characters was ASCII; the new standard is Unicode, with its huge expansion of the number of character slots. This new standard provides us with the possibility of creating fonts that contain many more characters than could be held in previous font formats; they can even contain several scripts – Latin, Greek, and Cyrillic, for example, all united in one font file. ‖ The PC (or Windows) system and the Macintosh operating system were not compatible – they were two different worlds. Both have the character of the 'de facto' commercial standard; but then with the proviso that the Windows world is so much more dominant than the Macintosh world (for reasons of tough business reality) that it makes the Macintosh world seem like an esoteric subculture. In the end the Macintosh operating system had to adapt, so that it could communicate better with other operating systems. With its OS-X, Apple made a move towards the Unix and Windows environments, providing a far better compatibility with the rest of the computing world.
‖ In these circumstances Adobe's Type 1 format was becoming simply useless, so it was time for a new Adobe font format; preferably one which could deal with Unicode. In another change of partners in the West Coast dance, Adobe and Microsoft joined forces to develop the new format of

OpenType. Hardcore font-engineers tend to regard OpenType as an of extension of TrueType — which means that it is based on a format that originated with Apple. 'At least they had the decency to make it an open standard', one commentator has written.* Microsoft had sound reasons of its own to develop OpenType. It allowed them to ease more fully into the world of Unicode and into a better way of doing non-Latin typography. Since these two companies have a great deal of power, OpenType looks like an industry standard. Although it is an open standard, it is still not really a cross-commercial standard. It is essentially a business deal between two companies. ‖ So OpenType provides an escape from PostScript Type 1 — into a situation that creates new possibilities for Adobe. It is a benign development, especially for the Mac-addicted graphic designer, who will also be better off with a workable compatibility between Windows and os-x: the same Open Type font file will run on both operating systems. But for the designer-maker of fonts the job becomes more demanding, as data-interpretation is removed from the users and their DTP packages and is put into the font itself. The days of the type designer who turns himself into a font-foundry may be over. ‖ To help sell the OpenType format in its Western markets, Adobe dressed it up with new features. These features make it possible to get a higher quality of typography more easily than is possible with Type 1. The number of font files can be reduced. Most obviously, you do not now need 'expert' or 'small cap' fonts. Small capitals and non-lining figures can all be stored along with the basic character set in one and the same font. Other micro-typographic features, such as ligatures, are also easier to access and use. Whether all this is going to be used in practice is still doubtful. If fi and fl are usually forgotten now, why should we suddenly start to use them with OpenType? But if the people who always wanted to use these subtleties are now better off, that is good. And for any script that makes heavy use of ligatures — Arabic or Devanagari, for example — OpenType's features become powerful and desirable. Arabic and Devanagari OpenType fonts are very good things.

My concern here is the font file: the thing that is sold to customers. This data package has certainly become more problematic, from the technical point of view. A lesson of Unicode and the OpenType format is that the maker of the font now has a more demanding job to do. To explain all this precisely, in technical terms, is beyond the scope of this essay; but it is fair to make the following comparison. Instead of a bicycle, we suddenly have to produce the much more complicated scooter. ‖ The managing director of Linotype, Bruno Steinert, said in his opening speech at the Heidelberg conference, that his company is not in the type industry any more. Over the years, typefaces have become commodities, and this has meant the end of the type industry. Now we are all in the font business. I can understand this argument, but I do not quite agree with it. I doubt whether you can call typefaces 'commodities' just like that. It is true that typefaces have been transformed from bulky masses of metal, which needed factory-halls for their production, and large store rooms, into files produced and stored on a single cd somewhere in a comfortable office. Type has lost the industrial character it still had even forty years ago. Already around 1900 the foundries were giving up their plain and neutral industrial type names, such as 'Gothic 237' or 'Clarendon number 3', and began to use commercially protected names such as Cheltenham or Souvenir. These brand names point to a very specific design (owned by a certain composing-machine manufacturer) rather than a certain version of some general category of letter. ‖ Although the industrial character of type has gone, this does not mean that you can wrap typefaces up as commodities, like ice creams – Hazelnut Crunch or Raspberry Ripple. You may open a little shop putting a colourful board outside saying ICE CREAM. If to the ices you add other commodities – candy-bars, newspapers, and French fries – you have a business; certainly if it is located between the parking garage and the shopping centre. But if you change ICE CREAM into FONTS you will probably be broke in no time. To survive in the market, commodities have to be wanted by the general public, to be easily accessible, and be based on a clear and uncomplicated 'business model'. This is not the case with typefaces. Typefaces, fonts — whatever you call them — do not have a clear and uncomplicated business model, as Bruno Steinert also stated at the end of the same conference, in a discussion about editable pdf files. If you treat your product just as a commodity when actually it is not one, then you get into trouble. ‖ When the internet arrived, the slumbering ways of the traditional type business were rather forgotten. With the internet, it seemed, you did not need a business model. With the fairy tale of a new economy that would push aside the old economy, the idea that typefaces can be regarded as commodities was promoted. Now, after the crash of the most fanciful 'dot com' enterprises, it becomes clear that the internet might have some effect on selling real commodities, such as books. If you buy a new title from Amazon, it's most likely that you became aware of the book's existence through a bookshop window, a review in a magazine, or a good friend whose opinion you respect. ‖ So it seems that in order to run an effective new economy, you need as much of the old economy as you can get. The internet gives you access to the entire world — yes, of course. But so does my front door. Having access and having a good business are two different things. It is doubtful whether you really need that much access in order to have a good business. The internet can be extremely effective for information, for finding details of things that you already know about in outline, such as the opening times of a museum or travel tickets. The internet is most powerful when used as a visual telephone. Collectors like it, and now they can roam the world in pursuit of their obsession. Users of type, however, have to have a proper look at a design, or at least to have heard about it from colleagues. They do not

search for unknown sites which might contain unknown typefaces to purchase. It is still through the old ways that they become aware of a certain typeface, and the fact that types are now little files of data, very suitable for transmission via the internet, does not play a significant part in the decision to use and to buy. Users might well obtain fonts via the internet, but only after the decision to acquire has already been made. The internet is then a delivery system, not a selling system.
‖ Again, the fact that a typeface can now be regarded and treated as a commodity does not mean that it really is a commodity. This could only be the case if it absolutely does not matter which typeface you choose. But very often the choice of a typeface is an important moment for the designer within the design process. The choice of a typeface is one of the skills of the profession. It can demand much attention and even testing. The process which defines this choice is complex. It does not have much to do with acquiring an off-the-shelf commodity in the blink of an eye. And the same must hold for the decision of a designer and even a producing company when they make a typeface.

* Thus Tom Arah in his article 'Type 1, TrueType, OpenType', online in September 2003 at <http://www.designer-info.com/Writing/font_formats.htm>.

Artisan or designer

I often find myself saying such things as: 'Well, this type design was made about four years ago when ...' Saying this, I often wonder: 'design'? 'make'? Am I a designer or a maker? It is a question that first cropped up twenty years ago when my teacher Alexander Verberne said: 'If you think out something and make it yourself, then you are a craftsman. If you have to make specifications for it, for someone else to execute your plans, then you are a designer.' ‖ So if I make some basic drawings of letters, add some notes, and give these to my assistant so that he can digitize them, this approach turns me into a type designer? If I did the work myself, because my assistant fell sick, then suddenly I am a craftsman? If we stick to this definition, then the first real type design might be the 7-line Pica Roman of the Flemish punchcutter Hendrik van den Keere.* Some of the wooden punches for this type clearly show the traces of pencil lines. But it is still not clear who was responsible for the actual cutting of the letters. It is possible that Van den Keere did the drawings on the wood pieces, then handed them over to one of his assistants, who then did the cutting. In this definition, the distinction between craft and design is a difficult one to make. Probably the formula is too much rooted in the industrial phase of the nineteenth and twentieth centuries, when a process was — much more than before or since — broken up into different steps of production. ‖ In the literature of typography, the Romain du Roi is considered to be the first type design — made in France in the years around 1700. Here the image of the letter was disconnected from any reproduction technique common in those days. Abbé Bignon's committee had to use this abstract approach because in fact their real aim was to come up with a model which excluded all the unclear and uncertain details that are unmistakably brought in by the hand of a craftsman. Take away these unclarities and doubtful details, replace them with all the rationality you can get, then the result will be the best possible one. It was an understandable line of thinking in the days when a rational approach was the new way to explore and — more important — to judge things. So that is why the Romain du Roi was displayed at rather a large size: so that we could have a clear look at it, with enough room for a grid, and the application of ruler and compass. Then we could really can see and thus test its rationality. This roman could then be regarded as a specification or sample for all the trades that use letters. ‖ Explaining letterforms with a ruler and compass is not new, not even in days long before the Romain du Roi. Albrecht Dürer is just one of several who can be used as a evidence of this. A difference between the approach of Dürer and the Bignon committee is that Dürer did not have an all-purpose letter in mind. The main group of his letters were capitals and some other sorts; traditionally these would be for ornamental use, for example in architecture. The Bignon committee however aimed at a norm for all letters. In my view this roman is not the first type design, but it is certainly the most complete approach of its kind. It is not only a complete proposal, it is also an entirely new approach to letters. It was pure and true, emotionless and universal (or if not universal, at least French). It was an approach that was condemned to fail, because universal letters cannot and do not exist. Despite that, in the case of the Romain du Roi there is in the end something really new, something which we can see now as a clear concept. It is the first complete conceptual proposal for letters. ‖ From this statement you can conclude that all the typefaces cut in the sixteenth century were the products of artisans. Robert Granjon had no clear concept when cutting his punches. He must have been sure of his thoughts and ways, but he kept these to himself, and they were certainly not on the table for discussion. Craftsmen and artisans can excel in technical skill, and when mature they often have their own specific signature or touch, and can indulge in playful variations. But in general they have no 'concept'. If they do have such a thing, it is a traditional one which they might

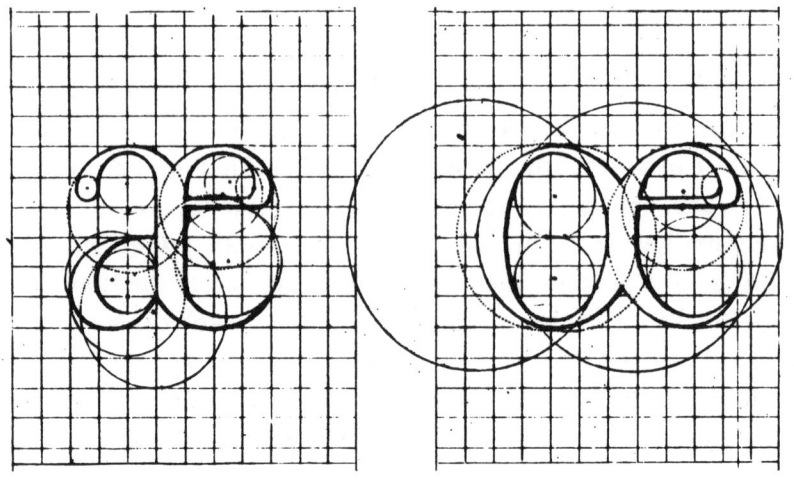

Glyphs from the Romain du Roi in the first set of plates engraved by Louis Simmoneau and dated 1695.

slightly improve or give their own twist to. But the general concept is usually a steady one: a standard evolved over the generations. ‖ Michelangelo's frescos in the Sistine Chapel do not have much to do with design, because he himself signed for the actual execution of the project: he was the artist or craftsman. So here we can also leave out the word 'design'? No, of course not. Michelangelo certainly designed the frescos of the Chapel as a whole, to be a unity. There is no doubt that there was much planning involved. Design implies not only a concept that has enough power to stand on its own, but it also often implies the necessity of a certain amount of planning. In general we have no trouble with the word 'design' in art, because creator, planner and executor are usually one and the same. The term 'craft' does not entirely cover this. Unlike the craft worker, it is assumed that a painter will come up with new compositions. In other words, the circumstances of each job will vary, and this is different from making the same wicker basket over and over again. ‖ This line of thinking can also be applied to type design and graphic design. Here industrialization has played a crucial role, making it necessary to divide the process into various mechanically determined stages. The people responsible for the visual outcome have usually also been the ones with a clear overview of the whole process. These people can be regarded as designers, certainly if they work outside a particular office or workshop, operating as freelancers and using the facilities of various manufacturers to achieve a cost-effective, well-planned, and beautiful product. ‖ Nowadays the tools are so powerful that the whole process has turned round and is often back in the hands of a single person who is designer, planner, and executor. And the various workshops of the old days are now unified in one machine called a computer. This is often true for general graphic design and for type design. But often now the line between artistic practice and design is difficult to draw. A good dictionary cannot be other than the result of a true design process. Yet it does not make much of an

impression, does not look flashy. It suggests rather the daily and down-to-earth activity called 'work'. No, the art catalogue is much more interesting to look at, is colourful, and makes a rich impression. The whole catalogue breathes an air of luxury; it is packed with tricks, with as many visual layers as the designer could get his hands on, to establish the continuation of his or her reputation among colleagues. I am sure that such an art catalogue took a lot of effort, taste and planning to produce, but it is difficult to call it design. It lacks a critical issue common to all design, namely plain judgement and testing. The catalogue is a luxury item that falls outside the common grounds of reason, cost-effectiveness, and serviceability. It is made to escape from this. ‖ You might as well ask yourself: is *haute couture* design? No, it is not; it is creation. Design is by definition open for general discussion. *Haute couture*, and modern art too, are fields that resist general criticism. Their existence is based on a luxurious exclusivity. The world of design is different. This does not mean that one is more or less than the other; they are simply different. Still, makers or designers need the same visual skills to create and then estimate the visual qualities of their work. What differs is not so much the level of creativity between the designer of *haute couture* and the designer responsible for the dictionary; what differs is rather the question of social responsibility.
‖ There are many fields that require creative talents, disciplines that require flexible minds which can come up with new concepts. Some of those fields carry great responsibility — the dictionary, the interface for a new software program — while other disciplines do not have to bother with these social responsibilities. There the responsibilities lie somewhere else, perhaps within the artists themselves. It is good to be clear about this: not to mix these things up, and to think that creativity is at its best in total freedom. There is a stupid tendency in design to make everything funny, to avoid trouble and effort, to escape from traditional views just because they set guidelines (seen as obstacles), and to

neglect responsibilities. And all this is only because of the misunderstanding that any 'applied art' cannot be really creative or new or highly conceptual. So the most mundane things are overdone, made up, with unnecessary and thus unclear concepts. Against all this nonsense, it becomes necessary to spell out the responsibilities which our creative talents have to meet. Do the job, as well as you can. Get on with it and keep quiet. ‖ Returning to type design: when one has to develop a sanserif family for corporate use, with variations of weight as well as of width, all with hand-hinting for better screen display, then you will need to take care of many factors in order to get a good result. It has to be possible to hint the typeface so that the resulting pixel-patterns of the condensed fonts look condensed compared with the normal variations in any situation. This needs planning. Nearly all the steps in type design constantly require a very high degree of visual sensitivity. A type designer needs this in order to judge his or her work right on the spot. Type design is loaded, soaked with responsibility. It is open to severe judgement over a very wide scale of detail and of time too – not just at the time of the reception when the new typeface was launched. It will have been judged constantly since its very beginning. A type designer cannot escape this responsibility of judgement, and there is little room for humbug. In the end, people – the society – either accept it or they don't.

* See also the discussion in my book *Counterpunch* (London: Hyphen Press, 1996, pp. 128-32), with its reproduction of this type – also available in H.D.L. Vervliet's *Sixteenth-century printing types of the Low Countries* (Amsterdam: Hertzberger, 1968, pp. 216-19).

Fifteen years of democratic type?

Type design is done by specialists called type designers. At least, that's what we may think at first. And it is true that there are many good typefaces made by 'real' type designers. But there are also many good typefaces made by people who mostly did other things, with some type designing on the side. By 'type' I mean indeed the letterforms used within typography, so I refer to the fonts which are used to compose text. This leaves out the area of handwriting, calligraphy, and lettering. Before the invention of graphic design, people who designed type might be engravers, writing masters, printers, or punchcutters. In the twentieth century many types were designed by people who had a strong relation to the printing industry but who were not type designers pure and simple. W. A. Dwiggins, for example, was a typographer and graphic designer who started to design type as well. Another example is the Dutch book typographer Bram de Does, who, after many years of working as a typographer, designed the typefaces Trinité and Lexicon. Both of these designers worked on typefaces that they themselves felt a need for, and these are often designs which excel in respect of drawing and character, within a certain style of letter. Another example would be Syntax designed by Hans Eduard Meier. Here a personal need to create a humanist sanserif made all the difference. What is important in these examples is that the designers started on the task out of a strong personal impulse; nobody asked them to do so.* ‖ Then there are the people who occupy themselves with type design and with nothing else. You will find them for sure in the world of the type-manufacturing companies: the employees working for Monotype, Adobe, or Linotype. In the factory — an office these days — people are asked to do type design or related activities for eight hours a day. They have to produce for the trade's sake, and within such companies there is usually not much room for one's own preferences and typographic needs. In addition to these opposite ends of the spectrum there are mixed cases. A company might ask a designer if he or she could provide them with a font. The request is often followed by some specifications from the customer; so *carte blanche* is rare in such a case. And which category – the individual or the industry – is responsible for the best work? It is hard to answer; the question is also not specific enough to be open to a proper answer. But the fact that it is difficult to answer shows that within type design the individual plays an important role. ‖ In the last decade and a half, more space than ever before has opened up for the individual type designer to work in. This, of course, follows from digital technology and the existence of easy and affordable font-design software. The software that can be used to design digital fonts is responsible for two important things. First, it has liberated type design, which used to be in the hands of the manufacturers that – and this was their main business – produced the composing machines. So type design has come within the reach of anyone who simply wants to design a typeface. Further, font-design software now contains within it the whole procedure of type design. The type designer does not depend on technicians any more. The whole process of design, as well as of production, can be done by the designer from one machine, from one desk, within one room. No more waiting for proofs which some technician has had to make for you, then making corrections, and again waiting for these corrected proofs. This indeed has an effect on speed: the procedure has become more simplified and efficient. With the process going so smoothly, font designers themselves have become more skilled, and the whole business has become more attractive. So students have learned quickly from these skilled people and, within a short time, the talented ones are becoming type designers. This also has a rather positive effect on production, resulting in an extensive growth of new designs of all kinds, as well as many so-called custom-made fonts. ‖ Nowadays a font can be designed in a few days or sometimes even less: much faster than in the days of

1. In former days the shape a new book was to take was a matter
2. In former days the shape a new book was to take was a matter
3. In former days the shape a new book was to take was a matter of

Le cortesie, l'audaci imprese io canto,
Che furo al tempo che passaro i Mori
D'Africa il mare, e in Francia nocquer tanto,
Seguendo l'ire e i giovenil furori
D'Agramante lor re, che si diè vanto
Di vendicar la morte di Troiano
Sopra re Carlo imperator romano.

Hans Eduard Meier and ?EL FOUNDRY in 1969. The humanist sanserif, in which ιre clearly visible. The italic, l, part italic, part sloped ;is will show that Syntax . The italic slopes at 11° and half a degree. Little as it is,

STEMPEL FOUNDRY in 1969. The roman is a true neohumanist sanserif, in which Renaissance forms are clearly visible. The italic, however, is a hybrid, part italic, part sloped roman. Close

gned by *Hans Eduard Meier* and issued by L FOUNDRY in 1969. The roman is a true st sanserif, in which Renaissance forms are

Trinité.
Lexicon.
Syntax.

photocomposition or hot metal. Or so it seems, if you look at what happens in this way. But is this the right way to look at it? With the new font-design software, new designs and custom fonts can be made in a flash. There are now many people around who open up someone else's fonts, change a few details, and — it's done. Is this type design? Another method that has appeared in recent years is to mix the designs you like, interpolate them between other good designs, and leave it at that; or perhaps they will change a detail here and there. It is an effective and very tempting method, especially for the newcomer, who will get convincing results with just a few clicks and keystrokes. But mixing or sampling is not designing, whether or not the result looks good or bad. The third method is to have a good look around and, as soon as something catches the market and your eye, then simply incorporate it into your own fonts. Just take the best from what is there and cover it with your own sauce. These are cunning font designers who know how it all works; they can handle the software effectively, but apparently that is the only thing they are capable of. Either they are too lazy, or do not have the time, or simply do not have the talent to do the job as it should be done. True, these guys have an eye for typefaces. But so have all my customers, who will start to say (as one of them actually did): 'New type designs? In general I do not bother with them. They all look the same: cheap copies, sampling. Why do they think I have time for stuff like that?' ‖ Digital technique enables people to mix and to sample. Music is a well-known victim of this, and type does not escape from it either. As I have said, the individual designer is important for type design. Today we have many individuals in the field. In fact, we have so many that you might wonder exactly how individual they are. As soon as an activity which used to be high profile gets a lower profile, then this usually means that more and more people are involved in this activity. This will always lead in the end to a devaluation. Suddenly there is so much of the same stuff around that it simply becomes a less interesting and a more

REAL
leather

REAL
leather

Above: Existing fonts can serve as the basis for logos, corporate slogans, and even whole 'new' typefaces. This method of working can never hide itself: the original will always be recognized eventually. Certainly when this process of making small changes is used to produce a whole font the result will be problematic, to say the least.

Opposite page, above: Blending different fonts can be a tempting way of making 'new' material. The large example at the top on the right looks like an average Garamond. In fact it is a mix generated automatically from Quadraat and Renard 3: at the top and the bottom in the smaller examples.

drainage

a mix

drainage

Quadraat

drainage

a mix

drainage

Renard roman 3

Typedesign
Typedesign
Typedesign

Another way to make new typefaces quickly: take an existing example (top) and then (second and third rows) play around with the strokes and terminals. It is often done with sanserifs. For the font boys it's a quick job, and often well paid by art directors who think they are buying a real, custom-made typeface. But by now the trick may have been done too often to be believed.

normal thing. Type design has become like graphic design: it has become democratized. There is nothing wrong with that. And, after all, that is what we wanted; we wanted more type designs and a more widespread interest in type. But there is a remedy against type designs which are not genuine enough, and against fonts (I refuse to call them type designs here) which simply borrow too much detail and character from other designs that paved the way for them just one or two years earlier. This remedy is — I am afraid to say it — taste. ‖ You may say, 'I do not care at all about taste'. The odds are that you do care about finance. Still, I've got a message for you. The three methods described above and illustrated with my own drawings (we try to stay polite) are typical of the present time. They occur with a frequency such as we have never seen before. We are used to speaking of type design, but clearly this term does not cover the whole field. So I would like to use this opportunity to introduce another term: font-tweaking. I think that there is a great difference between type design and font-tweaking, and this is interesting for a potential customer and especially for his budget. If you ever order a font, it is wise to make a clear distinction, to whomever it is you order from, between design and tweaking. The last illustration here ('typedesign') is a good example of a tweaked font. Something like this must cost at least 90 per cent less than a real custom design. Why? Because it makes use of existing data, and so there is no need to draw or to specify a design. There is no need to balance out the relations between the characters, or to justify the characters, or to make or place the accents, or to add and test kerning, and so on. It is all already there. The only thing done here was just to move around some points in an ambivalent way, and that did not take very long. So why would you ever pay for work which is already done? ‖ Yet I do not think that our present period is especially interesting. We seem to have an overdose: too much of the same. But even this is not new: it has happened more than once before. For example, it is possible to say that all the roman typefaces made in the sixteenth century are one big bunch of look-alikes. Only a handful of specialists could perhaps identify their punchcutters, by looking at book-pages printed in around 1580. It is easy to look at the sixteenth century from our perspective, to pack up a hundred years, and state that it all looks alike. Typographic material had to be available and it was not always possible to buy the material you needed, so you had to make it yourself or order it. Then the result might look the same, according to the standards of those days. But the makers of the types involved could not borrow instant skill, experience, or knowledge from others, as they can nowadays. It might look the same to you, but it was at least genuine. ‖ Or we might take a look closer to home. In the period between the two world wars, there was a peak in the design of sanserifs. It was possible to copy an image then, but still the capital, labour and competence had to be there too – so the copying could not be instant. Every company had its own variants, and often you have to read the caption to a specimen to know what you are looking at. Ludlow's Square Gothic would be an example. In general, this kind of design is all but forgotten, including some of the better ones, such as Tempo, also from Ludlow, or Stephenson & Blake's Granby. Some of these old designs show very contemporary features. Elegant from Stempel, Neon and Semplicita from Nebiolo, are examples. It is certainly in the nature of type design to provide such echoes. Of course this is something different from repeating the same tune straight away. ‖ Like much else, type design develops in waves. I do think that at the moment it has become inward-looking and even a bit incestuous. You may say: 'And what about you, Smeijers, you borrow and copy as well, do you not? Your Renard, for example, what about that?' My answer will be that I think there is nothing wrong with this typeface, because there are some essential differences here. First of all I do not hide where Renard comes from and who the real maker is. I say clearly that the source of the typeface is the 2-line Double Pica Roman, cut around 1570

**ENGINEERS TO 56
Alter plans for large
government project**

36 Point Ludlow 6-ZB Square Gothic — Length of lower-case alphabet: 521 points

**A STRIKING 58
Display face that
finds much favor**

96-Point Ludlow 28-BC Tempo Bold Condensed

**ADVERTISER 6
Reports largest
volume of sales**

96-Point Ludlow 28-HC Tempo Heavy Condensed

Opposite page, top: Square Gothic from Ludlow: one of many grotesques or gothics (the American term) in use in the early to mid twentieth century. Many of these typefaces have simply been forgotten, though the grotesque character is still to be seen in many current sanserifs, and the ubiquitous Helvetica and Arial show echoes of it.

Opposite page, second and third rows: Even large and well-planned families have not always lasted into later times and later technics. Tempo, from the Ludlow company, is an example of this. It was equipped with several variations of weight and width.

This page, above: Tempo even had had an italic variant with a more 'joyful' and casual character, made with the advertising market in mind.

PUBLISHERS
Gift Schemes
GRANBY 8pt. to 48pt.

MILAN HOSIERY
Stylish Designers
GRANBY CONDENSED 8pt. to 48pt.

AUSTRALIAS
New Ground
GRANBY BOLD 8pt. to 48pt.

ROMANCER
Island Home
GRANBY EXTRA BOLD 10pt. to 48pt.

CONVERTING
Desirable Loan
GRANBY LIGHT 8pt. to 48pt.

DEVELOPMENTS
Latest Enterprise

ELEGANT MEDIUM 8pt. to 72pt.

ABCDEFGHIJKLMNOPQRSTUVWXYZABCDe

abcdefghijklmnopqrstuvwxyz Das Leben der
ABCDEFGHIJKLMNOPQRSTUVWXYZ1234567

Opposite: The English typeface Granby, from Stephenson Blake, is an example of a sanserif that was well enough done but still did not survive beyond its time. The normal weight, especially, looks very familiar, even now.

Above: The fancy designs that often seem to be typical of recent times were often made years ago. The examples here: Elegant, which reminds us Emigre's Base Sans; Neon, an up-to-date 'lounge scene' single case alphabet, first issued in 1936; and Semplicita, which may remind us of typefaces such as Dax, but which was first issued in 1933.

a aaaa

software fácil y accesible para el diseño de fuentes. El software que puede utilizarse para el diseño digital de fuentes es el responsable de dos cosas importantes. En primer lugar, ha liberado el diseño tipográfico, que solía estar en manos de los fabricantes que también producían las máquinas de componer. Es como actualmente el diseño tipográfico está al alcance de cualquier persona que desee di-

En la actualidad, una fuente en unos pocos días, y a vece aun, mucho más rápido que fotocomposición o la comp O al menos así parece, si se lo que sucede de esta mane ¿es ésta la forma correcta d el nuevo software para dise den hacerse nuevos diseño:

By 1988, desktop software had become available to digitize typefaces. We took the original drawings and developed the typeface for use by our own studio, MetaDesign, and named the font Meta.

It took 'real' type designers to finish it: Just van Rossum, our first resident type designer, and later Lucas de Groot, who added new weights to the family. When we set a catalogue for FontShop, they liked it and persuaded me to license it. They released it as FF Meta and it quickly became a bestseller. The FF Meta family now has 81 members, including the condensed version and FF Meta

Top row: Garamond is by now a well-established category of typeface, as well as the name of the sixteenth-century French punchcutter. The first example here is a letter cut by Claude Garamond himself. Then letters from recent designs within the Garamond category: Adobe Garamond and Renard (both based on specific historical material), Lexicon and Quadraat (interpretations of the Garamond theme).

Second: Rubén Fontana's Fontana typeface.

Third: Erik Spiekermann's Meta typeface.

by Hendrik van den Keere. Second, just like the roman letters carved on the Trajan Column in Rome, the source is part of our common cultural inheritance. It is not owned by anyone and the creators have been dead for several hundred years. Third, the historical material was not there in a digital format, so the data is entirely — from the first to the last point — my own work. Last but not least, by making a revival of this Garamond-like typeface — one which has a very specific character of its own — I made the repertoire of classical typefaces richer. A reconsideration of tradition took place here, and Renard is a contribution; it is not just more of the same. It is clear that I am more in favour of echoing than of hitting the repeat button. ‖ Here I can touch on the question of 'revivals'. These are often decreed to be non-creative design. After all, they add nothing to development. But with true revivals there can be no intention of being creative, at least not in the limited sense used by those who dogmatically skim the horizon for something new. Making a revival has much to do with respect and understanding, and revivals require a great deal of skill. Enough professional colleagues have crossed my path boasting that they would never lay their hands on anything remotely resembling a revival. (So why is Quadraat Italic then an obvious source of inspiration for some of these people? It baffles me.) More than once they have had to bow and take a few steps back, or — let's put it more politely — they have changed their views and insights over the years. To be blunt, and it is good advice to serious newcomers: do not make the mistake of being afraid to be labelled 'conventional', 'traditional', or any other such dusty term. It is quite likely that one of your so-called 'traditional' typefaces is going to be used on the tombstone of the very design journalist who tried to put you into the unpopular dustbin, filled with conventional non-creatives years ago. And this macabre sentence grabs a lot of sense, probably more than the rest of this book put together. To tell the truth, new type designs are easy — like going to the toilet. It is the revival which really makes me sweat. Of course it is not forbidden as a type designer to refuse an interest in everything to do with revivals. But to me it sounds like the surgeon who can do any operation except the legs. ‖ There are also good things happening now, of course. We have type designs which, in my view, use or incorporate in a good way all the liberty gained over the last decade. An example of that is the Fontana typeface. This type design, which can be seen used in the Argentinian graphic design magazine *Tipográfica*, owes a lot to Meta and other sanserifs of a less complicated character from the last decade. But Fontana is not at all a Meta remake. It proudly travels further along the path opened up by Meta. Fontana is very uncomplicated, *très sympathique*, sunny, and open-minded; at the same time it is still serious enough to set long passages of text in, and somehow it mingles well with illustrations. It is suitable for daily work, and although it has some strong resemblances to other typefaces, the character of the whole is strong enough to let it be seen as its own thing. To some extent a tune is repeated here, but some years later, with some new couplets added and sung in a louder voice; and it is still pleasant to listen to. ‖ So Fontana is one of the good things that have come along in the last few years. But what is the future for designs such as this? A typeface is of course never an end in itself, not even for type designers. Type is there to serve humankind, and the goal of a typeface lies within this serving. A font used within the boundaries of present-day typography is in many respects nothing more than just a tool which enables you or anyone else to communicate visually. ‖ This fact is far more important than it may at first seem, because more people than ever are using fonts in order to communicate. Instead of speculating about type design, we might also ask ourselves: what are the tasks and duties of type now? The answer to this question could be that we need type so that we can use our computers. For computers, type is rather like the wheels of a car. No matter how sophisticated your BMW might be — with bullet-proof windows, air conditioning, and a satellite-linked navigation system — take away the wheels and it is useless. Now take away all the fonts from your computer and ask yourself what you can do with it then. A wheel is essentially simple and unchanged: it started with a circle, and it still does. And 'a' is still an 'a'. Of course, the wheel on your BMW is different from the wooden device attached to a medieval wagon. But we recognize both as wheels, and they do the same job; just as with a lowercase 'a' made by Jenson in 1485 and the 'a' of Fresco, a recent typeface. Certainly, the wheels of our cars have to meet many more demands than did its medieval ancestors — just as our present fonts do. ‖ In fact the type designs that we need most have not yet been made, or hardly so. The only truly adequate typefaces available are those that come with your system software. Suppose you are a big German insurance concern merging with a Russian company, and on the way you pick up a Greek business as well — you see the problem. Nowadays we need to have corporate identity typefaces in Latin, Cyrillic, Greek, and with all the East European accents, in Unicode and TrueType and OpenType, and hand-hinted. Most of recent type design simply does not measure up to these needs. But with more globally oriented communication in mind, we can say there are some good typefaces. Verdana, Georgia, Lucida, Arial and even Times can be useful. These typefaces may have huge character sets, but if this is all the decent typefaces there are, then our choice is rather limited. It reminds me of the early days of the Macintosh, with only a handful of fonts available: a sans, two or three seriffed faces, some display fonts, and of course a few fancy things. ‖ This kind of globally useful typeface requires much time to make, not just because it must support very big character sets. As well as more time, these require more skill and knowledge from their designers. In order to work well they have to be hinted, and hinting, as the illustrations here show, is well worth the effort. This process is simply a lot of work, and no matter how experienced you might be, it cannot go any faster. Some people say that it is all a matter of technique: the resolution of the screens has to be improved,

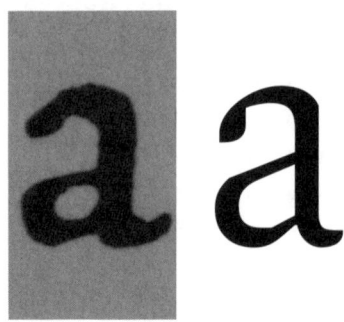

Making PDF documents accessible from the Macintosh Finder – PDF files created on Windows or UNIX systems will have a PDF icon and cannot be opene on the Macintosh by double-clicking. To enable doubleclicking to open the PDF files, do one of the following:

Macintosh by double-clicking. To enable double- clicking to ope the PDF files, do one of the following:
- Open the file on the Macintosh using File > Open or dragging tl icon onto the Acrobat Reader icon. After you have opened the fil on the Macintosh once, the next time the Finder redisplays the

Top row: The image of this Jenson letter was strongly shaped by the printing technique (letterpress) by which it was produced. The neighbouring letter, from the recent typeface Fresco, was made without any such technical context in mind. Five hundred years separate them, yet they both take their place comfortably in the conventions Latin script. We recognize both instantly as 'a'.

Second and third: To add manual hints to TrueType fonts in order to improve their on-screen quality is a complex and time-consuming activity. Hints not only ensure that the pixel patterns of characters in low resolution look neat, they also take care of the right spacing between characters and maintain the visual hierarchy within a type design: so that the bold looks bold and the normal looks like a normal weight. The picture shows exactly the same fonts, hinted and not hinted.

and that's all. Maybe, but I was sitting behind 300 dpi screens already in 1988. The technique needed for developing high-resolution screens has been there for more than a decade, but that does not mean it is available in the shops. If things stay as they are now, then an important part of the field of type design — making typefaces that are very widely usable — will be beyond the reach of the individual. Then this work will go again to the people who are sufficiently organized: the type studios of the manufacturing companies. ‖ Type design evolves unevenly, and the much proclaimed freedom of recent years seems to have a clear limit here. Whether this a real problem is hard to say, but I think that type designers should try to cross this border. Somehow it seems to me more worthwhile than fumbling around with someone else's serifs. But if individual type designers lose their grip on the ground gained in these last fifteen years then not much will have changed. These brief years will disappear into the history books: just as the days of dry-transfer lettering are now a matter of arcane knowledge. Then we also witnessed a sudden boom in all kinds of 'type' design, providing a legacy of typefaces that are hard to name now if the old Letraset catalogue is not at hand.

* You might say that Bram de Does does not quite fit this pattern. His first typeface came after he had been asked to adapt Jan van Krimpen's Romanée for photocomposition. In the end his answer to this question was a new typeface: Trinité. Trinité is a genuine design by De Does and far more suitable for photocomposition than Romanée could be; it can in no way be regarded as a photocomposition revival of that typeface.

The show goes on

Traditionally, type design was a rather closed activity. Newcomers were not always wanted and knowledge was sometimes kept secret. For example, the punchcutter Joseph Jackson learned many things by simply spying on his Caslon masters.* There is not much surviving evidence that points to factual knowledge transfer. Garamond was an apprentice of Antoine Augereau, and perhaps Hendrik van den Keere was a pupil of Robert Granjon, but clear beginnings and ends are rare. Where did Pierre Haultin get his knowledge from? As well as his punchcutting, he showed considerable knowledge and quality in the composing, organizing and printing of various books. Considering that these people were often on the run every few years, either from the plague, from religious persecution, or just the next war, it is hard to imagine how they managed to do all that they did. And it is probably just naive to think that in those days life was simple, merely because a graver uses no electricity and mobile phones were not yet invented. ‖ Verbal explanation, combined with demonstrating the required skills there and then, were probably the ways in which punchcutters taught each other the craft. All of this happened in a clear master–pupil relationship; at least until some of the skills began to be written down and published. Moxon's *Mechanick exercises* of 1683–4 was an early step in publishing some of the secrets. We are sure that knowledge was transferred, but this cannot often be traced back more than a generation or two. Thus the Fournier family of typefounders and printers may have run on for several generations, but we only really have knowledge of two of them. We are also aware of the fact that a craft such as punchcutting requires patience, combined with a strong personal desire or ambition, otherwise one will never succeed. These ingredients would also have led the real fanatics among them to keep on reinventing certain things. ‖ Self-education was, and is, very necessary too. But this is a very beautiful thing, or — better — a beautiful experience. One's own discovery of how to achieve something, or the invention of a certain skill or way of doing that solves a problem or speeds up a process for something one really cares about, is a very satisfying experience indeed. But this can lead easily to exaggerated self-belief, which in turn often results in an uncommunicative but very skilled craftsman: someone who believes that certain things cannot be done unless he himself has done them. On the other hand, after enough of these experiences, one can also start to look at things differently. When a craftsman, a punchcutter, faces a certain problem, the goals as well as the problem are clearly defined for him, and this is a help in finding the solution. With enough concentration and patience the solution will arrive. Knowledge and procedures were constantly reinvented, and to think that one is the first or even the best in a field is no more than naive. The so-called professional secrets were probably much more common knowledge than they liked to admit, or than we like to admit now. ‖ After the centuries in which the early punchcutters helped each other, or reinvented themselves over and over again, industrialization slowly took over the process. This meant one important thing above all: production became more and more separated from creation. The crucial break here came with the invention of the pantographic punchcutting machine, patented in the USA in 1885 by Linn Boyd Benton. With this device, and then with later developments of it, the implementation of the design became a matter making large-scale and very precise drawings that were translated automatically by a pantograph into smaller-size simulations of type. Identical punches and matrices could then be produced in the numbers that a power-driven composing machine might require. The drawings needed for the pantograph were technical ones, rather than artistic ones. The end of the process of separation was two completely different worlds. On one side there was the creative work, and on the other was the implementation of an idea. Or better, there was the type designer on one side, and the engineer on the other. The engineer and his staff were responsible for the complete translation of the designer's handsome drawings into the actual thing — type. ‖ The engineers were just solving problems that concerned the planning, the budget and the technology available. At least that is what we assume. But I am sure that some of these technical people were better type designers than the designers who just had to deliver an image: drawings indicating the general character and mood of the new typeface. The designers of that period, from around 1900 to the mid-twentieth century, were usually people who had tight connections to the graphic arts. It is the period that spans Oz Cooper and Roger Excoffon. Their knowledge in this field came largely from lettering activities, whether monumental, calligraphic, signing, or from fields more related to the printing industry — for example, the letters for a book-jacket or for an entire commercial advertisement. Those who excelled in this and became known might be asked by a typefoundry to provide a design. The message here is that in those days you first had to prove yourself as adequate before you were considered to be suitable for the job at all; you had to grow into designing type. Here one can add that it could help to have friends, who might introduce the designer to a typefoundry. And there was sometimes space for the talented in-house designer to emerge from within the ranks at the type company drawing office: Robert Hunter Middleton at Ludlow Typograph may be one example, Robin Nicholas at Monotype is another.

The use of letters and type, the exchange and use of written language, plays such an important role and is so much woven into our daily doings — much more so than even twenty or thirty years ago — that it is not strange that more and more people have become interested our topic. In the circumstances we have today it is hard to imagine that type design was once not liberated or democratized. Suppose that we had to live now with the lack of choice, freedom and flexibility in type that was there even as late as the mid-1960s. It's an impossible thought. But the nature of type accompanies changes in society; or perhaps it even precedes them a little, as was the case with digital type. This could be an example of a technical change that led on to some social changes. But my view is that when the social and cultural structure changes in a rather sudden way, then changes in the form and use of letters follow. As examples, think of Charlemagne's reform of script, the rise of sanserif in industrializing cultures, the Nazi edicts on letterforms, the spread of Cyrillic with the spread of Russian Communism. ‖ These days, in addition to the classes at The Hague, there are whole art-school and university courses that focus on type design. It seems strange that there should be structured courses in such a specialized activity, rather than in learning to create and work with letterforms more generally and widely. It looks as if there is a new global habit of making fonts from every letter-shape we may come up with — stash it into the character slots right away, generate a font, and look: you've made your own type. There may be nothing wrong with this, but have we figured out what is so good about it? ‖ Although in present circumstances graphic designers and typographers seem to drown in new font releases, there are still many professional users who are interested, and many young designers who spend time in studying type design. Maybe it is considered hip, I do not know. Certainly these courses provide insight into the matter, which is very helpful for any designer. On the other hand, even I cannot imagine producing six to twelve mature type designers every year. This is simply impossible. ‖ In such classes there is much focus on technique and procedure. For example, first you make an i, than you add a curve with an upright, from these two you make the n, turn it upside down and make a u, lengthen the first stem and create an h. The classes tend to concentrate on such basic stuff, and on knowledge that can be treated by the student as a recipe: do all this, in this and that order, and you will end up with a typeface. These strategies may produce usable fonts; but not (or not automatically) good type designs. Most of present-day production can be discarded right away. It is simply too much of the same thing. The fonts all breathe too much of the same shallow philosophy. These designs are real children of their time, and their contemporary-ness radiates from every detail. It is much too clear that a certain existing design has been taken as a mother font, or that too much inspiration has come from the teacher's own work.

‖ All this may sound rather harsh, certainly if one accepts that it is very normal for students to be influenced by their teachers. After all, a student has to grow and mature. That is true. But here the trouble starts. There seems to be no eye, not even any awareness of the need for this. It is as if visual judgement and discrimination do not count. A result is achieved; it works, and that seems enough — somehow there it stops. There is usually too little room for the courage to place it all in the real broader perspective. This starts with a lack of historical knowledge. It is rather easy to consider yourself original simply by ignoring the past — especially yesterday's past, so to speak. Then you do not know that a similar design has already been made.

‖ Letters and letterforms have always been made in large quantities — there is nothing new or special about this. There are now enough completely forgotten type designers, and even more forgotten lettering artists and designers who drew their own letterforms. Look at any fifty-year old survey and you will find them easily enough. It seems as if these things were less noticeable then than they would be now. Lettering was done for a specific job — maybe a book jacket with a run of 2,000 copies — and that was that. If you want to see these letters again you will have to know that the book jacket existed, then find an example of it. So the lettering was not used again. For the next job, the conditions were different and required another kind of lettering, or a similar but subtly different design. The limitations of those times required more hand-drawn letters. A designer had his own style or ways of doing it (Milner Gray, Helmut Salden or Susanne Heynemann would be examples). You could not easily copy the style – though you could imitate; that happened, of course. But nowadays as soon as some letters look good we immediately turn them into fonts, so that everybody can use them over and over again. So now there is a lot of 'digital lettering' going on. And very few designers make their own letterforms – well, maybe a logo now and then, but often this is just an adaptation of an existing font. If the lettering artists of the past were living today, they would be type designers too. ‖ Type design is not greater than mankind, but it is certainly greater than the designer, or – better – than a human life. It is very likely that Univers, like Gill Sans (you name it, there are many other examples), will be there for years after its designer, Adrian Frutiger, has died. Type design is inevitably tied up with its past, and I do not care about all the charlatans who popularly claim otherwise. A profound understanding of the essence of type design – its nature – would probably scare off a lot of students. But at least the ones who really want to work would stay. As history also shows, there are and there always will be new candidates. ‖ This might imply a conservative or stiff attitude. That is not how I think of it. But I try to avoid wasting time with popular nonsense. It is not necessary to dress things up to look more attractive than they really are, especially when you are teaching students who have made a real commitment of time and money for their education. They have the right to know what it is that they are entering. No matter how light-hearted you are, and although there is always enough to do, a designer's life – a type designer's life too – does not come for free. ‖ Against my words we might place Matthew Carter's, from an interview he gave with a magazine: 'There are a lot of young type designers who make better type than I did when I was their age'. That is an honest and open statement. But the meaning here is not so much that these young designers are suddenly more gifted. Rather his remark points to the fact that present possibilities are far more generous, both technically as well as economically, for the reasons that I have already given. ‖ Today type design has the chance to free itself from its image as a closed and inward-looking activity which stands more or less on its own. Type design stands with both feet in the middle of our society. It is more than ever an applied art that is there to serve all the other applied arts; a design discipline that is there for all the other design disciplines. And it is certainly not a static phenomenon.

* Talbot Baines Reed reported on punchcutting at the Caslon foundry in Chiswell Street, London: 'This was kept a profound secret at Chiswell Street, Caslon and his son locking themselves into the apartment in which they practised it. Jackson, who had a great desire to learn the mystery, bored a hole through the wainscot and was thus, at different times, able to watch his employers through the process, and to form some idea how the whole was performed; and afterwards applied himself at every opportunity to the finishing of a punch.' (*A history of the old English letter foundries*, ed. A.F. Johnson, London: Faber & Faber, 1952, p. 310.)

A new moral code?

In typography, one success is never enough. Letterforms, if they catch on, will become 'types' of a certain letter, and are regarded by society as normal. And then they are a matter of general culture – yet at the same time they may still be somebody's creation, and their name may be the property of a manufacturing company. With a broad category of letter, such as grotesque or sanserif, one typeface is soon not enough, and competing foundries start to make similar designs. The problem is as old as typography itself, but it is also not a static one. From the early days we might think of Aldus Manutius, who suffered from people copying his style of books and letters. However unfair and distressing such pirate behaviour might have been, it was also unstoppable and irreversible too. As typography grew in its effects and importance, this problem slowly became more prominent, until the moment when attempts at regulation began to be made. ‖ When, in 1957, the Association Typographique Internationale (ATypI) formulated its 'moral code', it was an attempt to deal with this paradoxical problem. The main players in this organization were the typefoundries. For as long as typefaces were tied to a particular composing machine, they were the only ones who were capable of transferring a design into type. With the formation of ATypI, the foundries decided to try to behave acceptably towards each other. The code was in part an attempt to establish how and when a design could be copied: after 'an appropriate space of time', as the document of 1957 put it. These producers were competing, but they each had solid shares of the market, and their world was still moving slowly. Type designers had a place, but it was on the sidelines. Since then the world, including the world of type, has been changing at an ever increasing speed. ATypI's code soon fell into disregard, even among the manufacturers who had supported it. And now that the club of manufacturing companies has lost its power, and now that type is made and

sold in quite other ways, the whole matter must be rethought.
∥ A moral code aims at a certain kind of protection: protection from other human beings, or even from ourselves, from our behaviour in relation to a specific object — in this case type. (It is not necessary here to define what a typeface is.) As far as I know, ATypI's moral code never worked or had any substantial effect on behaviour. Since with time and technological change things seem only to get harder to grasp, it is tempting to say 'let's forget about it, it's too complicated, everything has changed far to much'. I think this is not the right way to go. True, things have been changing and will continue to change, and probably at great speed too, but meanwhile we are getting quite used to the new situation, and probably the most essential changes have now happened (for the time being). It is true that a moral code is a nice idea — but what is the use if it has no real power? ∥ In my opinion the answer is quite simple. A moral code will never protect you from the really bad guys, and it is wrong to assume anything of that kind. A moral code provides in the first place a platform for judgement and behaviour, so that at least the bad guys can clearly be identified and labelled as such. The crucial changes of recent years created a vacuum. The old ones forgot about their behaviour, or did not realize how much was still true and good about it. After all, they had to adapt too, in many ways, otherwise they would not survive. At the same time the gates have been opened for newcomers who do not know how to behave, or pretend not to know. Open spaces are quickly filled by the disrespectful; the neutral zones are conquered by the brutal ones, as soon as they think this suits their needs. Grey areas are then said to be to be white; bad habits are declared to be legal. This will go on and on. Many things now happen which are simply unacceptable. The possibilities provided by the new techniques are not an excuse here. We are all too busy grabbing our share of the market. We can hope that less prosperous times will turn our minds away from our bank accounts a little, to allow an atmosphere in

which we are willing to think about what it is we are doing. The misbehaviour that is now allowed, with a shrug of the shoulders, is accepted as normal by the younger ones. At the moment we are completely floating. So a moral code provides guidelines for behaviour. This is good for all who agree to respect the guidelines, and is a way of introducing newcomers to the field. It gives us, at least, the opportunity to point with a finger. ‖ There are three parties involved: type designers, manufacturers and distributors, and the user or the customer. The ideal is a moral code drawn up by an organization so powerful that it could prevent other organizations and even companies from doing the wrong thing. But it's a fantasy. ‖ Much of the trouble with the companies is that they are often dealing in the grey area of possibilities opened up by technology, with which the law or even moral standards are not used to dealing. In a nutshell: technology can be developed so fast, stimulating ways of acting and behaviour with such a speed that it is impossible for moral standards and the law to keep up. Duelling with large organizations that have major interests is difficult and should be left to other powerful organizations. However, the most powerful force is the mass of the unknown consumer or user. A moral code should therefore focus in the first place on the individual. As I have been saying, type plays an important role in our Western society. So maybe a moral code should work from the bottom up, rather than top down. The moral code of an organization like ATypI should not focus on the interests of their typical members — the type designer or manufacturer. It should focus rather on the largest group it can reach. This is not the group of its members, nor yet the people in the street still using Windows 97. But it may be the world-wide community of designers and their organizations. ‖ There is a new world now, and there is no way that any moral code will touch the ways in which this new world operates. If something is convenient and can be done on a large scale, it will happen, no matter what. So any code will fail if it is too focused on itself.

Type is so woven into daily patterns that you have to take into account the many other factors that help to shape it — which is a hindrance in defining a clear moral code. The problem can be solved by bonding with other groups of professional users of type. See what interests you share, and out of that process define a code, to create a stronger voice which might be heard. ‖ Professional users of type are people who are active in the applied arts. These arts have general rules that have evolved over the centuries: rules rooted in honesty, honour, skill, and an atmosphere of respect for individual creation. These unwritten rules cover the same general principles, no matter if you are an architect, a sculptor, or a designer. The developments of the last two decades seem to have had a disconnecting effect, severing us from these rules. It does not really matter what you are designing, there is still a rule which says that copying is not allowed, not true, dishonest — certainly if you do not credit the original source. ‖ We have to go back to such down-to-earth first principles, before we make it more complicated. It is already difficult enough in these days in which the technical developers openly state that the 'original' does not exist. This is tricky. Since you are a designer, you smile at these words, because the original lies in your archive drawers. Does it really? Come on, ninety per cent of your work does not need any paper at all. And if it does, these are just rudimentary sketches, visual thoughts, which could be made by anyone. If the original does not exist any more, then technique wins over man. And we all know that creation starts somewhere: it starts in the trained minds of creative people and not in machinery. It is an intellectual thing. It is the designer's thoughts visualized. But how to protect thoughts, and how to prove that you are the one who thought them first? ‖ Apart from the really bad guy, our real enemy is the speed of change. Things change so fast that we do not really care what is going on anymore. We even come to expect surprises. It is impossible for formal agreements to keep up with this. And even if they could, they would not be of much use, since you

would not know when the agreement had changed. The only anchor-point in the whole scene is the thing that changes the least, and also the thing that is most important. The answer to this riddle is simple: as I have said, it is probably us — we, the human beings — who change least. Normal, easily applicable and understandable rules need to come back and to be advocated again. These rules should apply not only to the world of type but to the world of the typographer and the graphic designer. If you say that this is not possible, then I have to think that you put technology before yourself.
A young reader may sigh at these words, or think that it does not concern them — the young and hip ones. Well, enjoy these days, because the time is moving fast, and the young ones grow old, faster than ever before. ‖ If all this makes sense, what then are the rules?

A code of conduct

These are some general guidelines for conduct in the many disciplines that work with music or sound, with words, with drawings, diagrams and photography. All of these disciplines can be considered as design activities. So this code is addressed to designers, especially those of the digital generation.

0. Why take the first step of making something? It must come from an urge to create. If you set to work merely to make a cynical copy, then you lose the basis of design.

1. A design is considered to be the outcome of a creative process. This outcome is considered to be an original. But often this is not really the case. The designed object is a compilation of a number of things, with contributions made by others as well as by the designer. For example: a book about a photographer.

2. In order to claim a design, it should therefore always be clear who is responsible for what. Or, if this is not possible or necessary, you should be specific about your role in it.

3. There is almost nothing that is free of copyright. Be aware of the fact that everything has been created by someone other than you. The excuse of 'I found it on the Web' (as if it was a gift from God) is not valid.

4. When something is used frequently, or is simply very old, this does not mean that it is in the public domain. What is or is not 'public domain' is certainly not for you to decide.

5. Usually, for everything that has been made by another person, even in another discipline, money has to be paid, acknowledgements have to be given. It is good to realize that nothing is really free, not even your own snapshot taken in the museum — even though it was your fingers and your camera that made this photograph. You may put a print of your photo

of the Holbein picture on the wall of your living room, but do not publish it in a book without permission of the museum that looks after it, and pays for its preservation.

6. Copying and borrowing are easier than before. This is not bad by definition. Copying for study purposes is OK, but you can not label such things as your original design, and you must give credit to the original owner/creator.

7. Adapting and using somebody's else design work without any permission is unworthy of you, unprofessional, and will be bad publicity in the long run.

8. A situation might arise in which you have to slightly adapt an existing design. This can be done only if the creator has given permission for it, and if the owner of the design — the original customer who ordered the work or the present rightful owner — asks you to do the adaptation. If the original creator has not given or will not give permission, for whatever reason, then it is better to stay away from this kind of muddled situation. You cannot claim an adaptation as your design.

9. Worse than this is to claim someone else's work as yours — however much you might adapt it — and then give it away for free, or sell it publicly. This is still called piracy and you might face legal consequences.

10. When you leave a company and start your own design business, you cannot take that company's software and typefaces, or its stock photography, just because they have already been paid for. You can share costs with other designers in a small studio: the rent, a printer, a fax machine, and so on. But you cannot share the costs of software and other copyrighted material: just as a client of yours cannot — without asking you — sell your work to some other company.

And note further:

1. Who decides whether something is in copyright or not? There are laws and precedents to which we agree to defer, and which may vary from country to country, continent to continent. They can be tracked down and read.

2. It is helpful to bear in mind the claims and rights of the various parties here. Design must be regarded as intellectual property. So Adrian Frutiger is the rightful creator and intellectual owner of the Univers design. But the name 'Univers' may be established as a trade mark by some other party — for example, Linotype. So nobody can name a new type design 'Univers' just like that, not even Frutiger himself. On the other hand, Linotype cannot change the Univers design — Frutiger's intellectual property — without his permission. There is a third party here: the user. Someone who acquires a license to use Univers can have nothing to do with the design or its name. The user's rights are those described in the license agreement, nothing less and nothing more. So, in general, users never own copyrighted material, but are only granted the right to use it, as described in the license agreement.

3. Student designers, their teachers, and the people who run educational establishments, are no less exempt from these guidelines than are designers 'in the real world'.

4. These are clear and understandable rules, but more than ever a designer or a design organization should also consider the consequences of their activities for the client. My practice tells me that many clients want to be legally correct; they do not want to take any risks. In fact they often want to be more correct in what they do than the freelance designers they hire. Design is not confined to printed products alone, and these days the client's office will be scattered with computers. So, for example, you (graphic designer) cannot ask me (type designer) to make a Windows version of the typeface you used for TransOcean's corporate identity, when they say they need a couple of CDs with all the fonts and templates for their offices in Brazil. The larger your client, the more important it is that

the designers are fully aware of the consequences of the steps the client wants to take with the new design. You might design wonderful forms and nice brochures, but what if these are to be downloaded by anyone from the client's server — to save printing costs or just to be more accessible for anyone in the company who might need copies? In such a situation, you cannot just take and use anything from your own or somebody else's hard disc, at least not without considering what the proper price for this will be. The moral here: as a designer not only is it wise to consider what, how and from where you take your design ingredients, but it is equally important to be clear about the ways in which the design will be used by the clients themselves.

Glossary

These are among the names and the terms in this book that seem to demand explanation. The explanations are intended as a help especially to students now, and to readers in a future in which this knowledge may be obscure. We have drawn information from, and checked against, a wide variety of sources: accumulated experience, conversations with colleagues, books and journals, the World Wide Web. All of it is, of course, open to discussion. RK

|| **Adobe** Adobe Systems Incorporated. Software company founded in 1982, in Mountain View (California), by John Warnock and Charles Geschke. Their first product was the PostScript page description language, and their money came from royalties on licenses for the use of PostScript in printers and other output devices. With the coming of 'desktop publishing', Adobe began to develop and sell software packages, and became a serious player in the production of typefaces, including new designs of its own.

|| **Apple** Apple Computer Incorporated. Founded in 1976 by Steven Wozniak, Steven Jobs, and Ron Wayne, in Los Altos (California), and incorporated in 1977. The company began to enter the realm of typography in 1984, with the launch of its first Macintosh computer. The Mac's 'graphical user interface' helped to make possible typography on the small computer.

|| **ASCII** American Standard Code for Information Interchange. A code in which each alphanumeric character is represented as a number from 0 to 127, translated into a 7-bit binary code for the computer. Extended ASCII has additional characters (128–255). ASCII is used by most small computers and printers, and text-only files can be transferred easily between different kinds of computer platform. The limits of ASCII become apparent when used to represent languages outside the core American and European set.

|| **ATypI** Association Typographique Internationale. Founded at a meeting in Lausanne in 1957, the initial impetus for ATypI came from the typefoundries: it was to be a forum for regulating their industry, especially over the vexed question of copyright in typefaces. To this end a 'Code Morale' was drawn up for members. Later, designers and teachers began to be allowed a place in the organization too. As the technics of typography has changed, so ATypI has moved to being simply an international club for type people, with annual meetings in interesting locations.

‖ **Augereau** Antoine Augereau (c. 1485-1534). Printer and punchcutter in Paris, said to have taught Garamond.

‖ **character** A letter, numeral, or other discrete sign – the single elements that are used to compose text. In computer terminology: 'an encoded element of text'. See also 'glyph'.

‖ **character set** Traditionally: the set of characters in a font. So one would refer to the character set of Times Bold Italic. Now that we make the distinction between glyphs and characters, the term might rather be 'glyph set'.

‖ **commodity** In his book *Das Kapital*, Karl Marx defined the special sense that now attaches to this word: things become commodities when they are sold or exchanged. Water sold in bottles is a commodity; flowing freely in a river, water is not a commodity. So 'commodity' refers to exchange-value, and has no bearing on use-value. Whatever their politics, modern commentators echo this understanding of the word, and this is the sense of it in the present book.

‖ **Cooper** Oswald Cooper (1879-1940). Lettering artist and type designer in Chicago. In the 1920s he designed a series of typefaces, the best-known of which is Cooper Black.

‖ **digital** A loose word, but in the phrase 'digital type' it means that the descriptions of the characters of a font are stored as information in a digital computer. On this definition, digital typography really started with the CRT (cathode ray tube) typesetting machines of the mid-1960s.

‖ **dpi** Dots per inch. The unit used to describe the resolutions of an image produced by a printer or monitor.

‖ **DTP** Desktop publishing. Originally (1985), the idea of personal computer users becoming their own typesetters and printers, by means of a small computer, page-make-up software, and a laser printer for proofing or final output. Now, as in the phrase 'doing the DTP', it means 'doing page make-up on a small computer'. The term is credited to Paul Brainerd, the man behind the PageMaker software and founder of Aldus Corporation, speaking in January 1985 at the annual general meeting of Apple Computer Inc.

‖ **Dürer** Albrecht Dürer (1471-1528), the greatest German artist. His theories of letterform proportion and structure were published within his general book on measurement and proportion: *Underweysung der Messung mit dem Zirckel und Richtscheyt* in 1525. The text is known especially through the Grolier Club edition, *Of the just shaping of letters* (New York, 1917, reprinted by Dover Publications, New York).

|| **Excoffon** Roger Excoffon (1910–83). Graphic designer in Paris, with a speciality in type design, notably for the Fonderie Olive in Marseille, to which he was a consultant through the 1950s.

|| **font** With hand-set metal type, a 'font' in English was a set of characters of any one size and style: say, 8 point Baskerville Italic. In this example the 'type' or perhaps 'typeface' was Baskerville. Such a font was given a price and each font could be bought separately: so one could buy the 8 point italic without the 8 point roman. With the coming of typesetting that generated multiple styles and sizes from a single set of master characters, this distinction broke down. 'Types' (which had meanwhile become 'typefaces') now became 'fonts'.

|| **format** The way in which a font description is programmed by a particular manufacturer.

|| **Garamond** Claude Garamond (c. 1480–1561). Punchcutter in Paris. His name now attaches to a category of typeface: one that follows the forms of types cut by him and his associates — 'distinguished by their graceful proportions and brilliance of cut' (Harry Carter, *A view of early typography*, London: Oxford University Press, 1969, p. 84).

|| **glyph** Used now in distinction to 'character', to mean the visible forms that are used to display encoded text. For example, the characters 'f' and 'i' may be representable in some typefaces by a single glyph: the fi ligature. In scripts other than Latin ones, the relation of characters to glyphs is often complex.

|| **Granjon** Robert Granjon (1513–90). Punchcutter and printer in Paris, Lyons, Antwerp, Rome. Can be ranked with Garamond as a master punchcutter of that time. See, most recently: H.D.L. Vervliet, 'The italics of Robert Granjon', *Typography Papers* (Reading: Department of Typography & Graphic Communication), no. 3, 1998, pp. 5–59.

|| **Haultin** Pierre Haultin (c. 1510–87). French punchcutter and typefounder. A strong Protestant, he was active in Paris, Geneva, and elsewhere. His types are remarkable for their economy and 'to-the-pointness'. See, most recently, the two-part article by H.D.L. Vervliet: 'Printing types of Pierre Haultin', *Quaerendo*, vol. 30, no. 2 & no. 3, 2000, pp. 87–129, 171–227.

|| **hinting** The technique of achieving optimal character shape at small sizes and on low-resolution output devices. Without this intelligent compensation, characters will appear ill-formed.

‖ **justification** The word has two distinct senses in typography. As in this book, it refers to the process by which the image of a single character is fixed and defined within its field, along both horizontal and vertical axes. For some discussion of this in the days of punchcutting by hand, see Smeijers's *Counterpunch*, chapter 15, 'Fixing the image'. The other sense of 'justification' refers to the process of adjusting the spaces between words, so that the lengths of lines of text appear equal.

‖ **Van den Keere** Hendrik van den Keere (c. 1540-80). Punchcutter in Ghent, who became the sole supplier of type to Plantin's office: 'his importance cannot easily be overrated. He is the link between the French school which dominated the sixteenth century and the Dutch which led Europe for a century after it.' (H.D.L. Vervliet, *Sixteenth-century printing types of the Low Countries*, Amsterdam: Hertzberger, 1968, p. 32.)

‖ **Latin** In this book, as in the phrase 'Latin script', the word means 'using the letters of the roman alphabet' — as distinct from Greek, Cyrillic, Arabic, or any other such system of conveying linguistic meaning visibly.

‖ **ligature** Two or more characters combined as one glyph.

‖ **Microsoft** Incorporated. Software company founded in 1975 in Seattle (Washington) by Paul Allen and Bill Gates. Microsoft began to grow to its present position of dominance with the contract from IBM for an operating system for its personal computer. This became MS-DOS (Microsoft Disk Operating System), issued first in 1981, and also marketed independently from IBM by Microsoft. The successive versions of the Windows interface, built onto MS-DOS, helped to consolidate the company's position of near-monopoly in personal computing system software.

‖ **Noordzij** Gerrit Noordzij (b. 1931). Dutch writer (in all senses), typographer, and teacher at the Hague Royal Academy of Art (1960-90). As a graphic designer, his main client was the Amsterdam publisher Van Oorschot (from 1978). His principal writings are *The stroke of the pen* (1982), *De streek* (1985), *De handen van de zeven zusters* (2000), and the informal bulletin *Letterletter* (1984-96). A bibliography of his writings, and writings about him, is online (in September 2003) at <http://letterror.pctr.com/noordzij/index.html>.

‖ **OpenType** A font format developed jointly by Adobe and Microsoft, in a collaboration first announced in 1996. OpenType is based on the previous font technologies of TrueType, PostScript and GX. An OpenType font file can contain TrueType glyphs or PostScript outlines. Like Apple's GX, it uses

63

Unicode's large character set, and is thus much more workable for non-Latin scripts than Type 1 font files. The first OpenType fonts were released in 2000.

|| **OS-X** Apple's tenth Macintosh operating system, released in 2001. Based on Unix, it shows greater stability and efficiency than the previous versions of the Macintosh operating system.

|| **PC** Personal computer. In its primary meaning: a computer used by one person at one time. Here, as has become customary in recent years, it is used to mean an IBM-compatible computer that runs on MS-DOS/Windows, as opposed to Apple Macintosh computers. The first PC, from IBM itself, was launched on the market in 1981.

|| **pdf** Portable Document Format. Adobe's file format which represents a document independently of the software and hardware used to create it: it can thus be used across different computer platforms.

|| **PostScript** Adobe's page description language into which images are converted. Fonts are treated like any other graphic element, so that operations like rotation or screening can be applied to text too. PostScript descriptions are independent of output resolution and can run on any device that has the necessary software installed. It was that, especially, that changed the way in which typography worked: typefaces were no longer tied to particular machines, and could be made by one-person producers.

|| **Romain du Roi** The most visible and enduring outcome of the great project, conducted by a group led by the Abbé Bignon, and under the auspices of the French Académie des Sciences, to investigate and describe the art or craft of printing. The first engraved plates of the letters of what became known as the 'Romain du Roi' date from the 1690s. See, most recently: James Mosley, Sylvie de Turckheim-Pey, & others, *Le Romain du Roi: la typographie au service de l'état, 1702–2002*, Lyon: Musée de l'Imprimerie, 2002.

|| **script** One can distinguish two senses of the word in typography. As in this book, it means a visible system of conveying linguistic meaning: 'Arabic script' or 'Latin script'. The English word 'script' (unlike its cognates in other European languages) is used to distinguish written from typographic letters, and thus a 'script typeface' is one that imitates written forms.

|| **sort** A term from metal typography: a single piece of type. Used especially in the phrase 'special sorts', which were characters or elements outside the normal set.

|| **Spiekermann** Erik Spiekermann (b. 1947). German graphic designer, type

designer, writer. As a designer his main activities have been with MetaDesign, the practice he set up in 1983 in Berlin, and which he left in 2000. With Joan Spiekermann he established the typeface distributor and publisher FontShop International. Among his typefaces are ITC Officina (1980) and FF Meta (1991). His principal writings are the books *Ursache & Wirkung* (1982) – in English as *Rhyme & Reason* (1987) – and *Stop stealing sheep* (1993).

|| **standard** Derived from the Latin word 'extendere' (to stretch out), it came to mean a flag, around which people could rally. From this comes its meaning as a thing fixed by authority or agreement to serve as a level of quality. With industrialization, standards have become the subject of national, international and cross-commercial agreement.

|| **TrueType** A font format developed by Apple, in association with Microsoft, in rivalry to Adobe's Type 1 format. Like Type 1 it works with scalable outlines, but which are described by simpler maths and which allow superior hinting. First released in 1991.

|| **type** In hand-set metal typography: the pieces of metal bearing the image of a character. It may be strictly meaningless to speak of 'type' in non-metal typography; certainly the metal sense of the word has to be generalized.

|| **typeface** The image of a character on the face of a type: a particular set of characters constitutes a typeface. The term came into its own with the design and marketing of named types, from around 1900. See also 'font'.

|| **Type 1** PostScript Type 1 is the font format developed by Adobe, and launched in 1984. Characters are defined as outlines rather than the bitmaps previously used in digital type. Unlike Adobe's Type 3 format (there was no Type 2), this format supports hinting. The specification for Type 1 fonts was at first kept secret by Adobe, and published only in 1990.

|| **Unicode** An international standard for representing characters. Its 16-bit encoding of characters allows the representation of 65,536 characters instead of the 256 of Extended ASCII. Developed by the Unicode Consortium, which is composed of industry representatives but is non-profit making. See <www.unicode.org>.

|| **Unix** Computer operating system devised from the late 1960s onwards, mainly at Bell Labs in the USA. As the name suggests, it was an attempt to provide an operating system that could be used by computers of all kinds and sizes. It is open-source: its core components are freely available.

|| **Verberne** Alexander Verberne (b. 1924). Dutch typographer and teacher at

the school of art in Arnhem. Best known for his design (with Ton Raateland) of *Range*, the Philips house magazine, and of W.Gs. Hellinga's book *Kopij en Druk in de Nederlanden / Copy and print in the Netherlands* (1962).

|| **Windows** Microsoft's 'graphical user interface' for PCs. Announced in 1983, the first version of Windows was put on the market in 1985. This and the successive versions of Windows have often been seen as an effort to catch up with the Apple Macintosh interface; though this history is complex and has been the subject of much debate.

Typefaces

The pages that follow show a selection of typefaces designed by Fred Smeijers. We have tried to show them appropriately, using a text of real content for the serious text typefaces here, with some outbreaks to show the display typefaces. Our text is part of a work published in 1567 by Christopher Plantin in Antwerp under the title *Dialogues françois pour les jeunes enfans*. We give here the whole of the dialogue on writing and printing. Plantin's book has its text in French and Flemish on facing pages. Our English text is the translation by Ray Nash, which was the centre-piece of the book *Calligraphy & printing in the sixteenth century*, edited by him and published in 1964 by the Plantin-Moretus Museum in Antwerp. That book gives the pages of the original in facsimile, has extensive notes by Ray Nash, and an introduction by Stanley Morison. Nash reports that only two copies of the book of 1567 are known to exist, and both are in the Plantin-Moretus Museum. For further discussion of Plantin's dialogue on writing and printing, one must turn to Nash's book, to which we are indebted for what is said here, as well as for the gift of its translation.

There are three speakers: G, H and E. The piece is introduced by G. While it is supposed that Plantin himself may be the author of this work, whoever wrote it speaks in the voices of three men, each of them fairly surely identifiable. The layman, G, was the physician and poet Jacques Grévin, who was the general editor of these dialogues. The expert on writing, H, was probably Pierre Hamon, secretary to the young Charles IX and author of what is said to be the earliest French book on formal writing. The expert on printing, E, was probably Robert Estienne, printer to the King of France and the most celebrated member of that family of printers.

RK

CALLIGRAPHY AND PRINTING / DIALOGUE

G·H·E·

69 Denda New (Denda New Bold Condensed)

I have often marvelled, and with reason, at the great industry of men who, knowing their limitations, in that they cannot be at the same time understood by one another and be taking part in all that is done and said by the countless people of the earth, have nevertheless found out the greatest secrets so that in an instant they can know all that is done and also be understood, even throughout an age, by as many men as the different regions sustaining them. They have done this not only to know the conduct and handling of matters arising within their lifetime but also to understand things which are past, in order to pass them down to those who should survive them and to portray them as they are to their successors, who by this means can see after a thousand years the things which were done as if they had been present. It is all the more marvellous that this thing seems an approach to immortality. For man, who is himself not immortal, except as to his soul, by this means has in a manner transcended his ordinary destiny, though still prevented from going beyond the boundaries laid down for him by nature. So it is as though wings were put at his sides and he could fly aloft and raise himself so high that everyone could see him. He is also, as it were, freed of the debt which we naturally owe to death, so much so that by this means he can live as long as the world shall exist. This deep secret, however, is nothing but writing, which being like the picture of words and consequently of the fears, comprehensions, discourses, judgments and reasonings of men, has none the less the virtue of representing them, whenever we please to glance at it. Considering these matters one day, walking by myself outside the city, I happily met two of my good friends: one the finest scribe of our times and the other the most diligent printer there has ever been, both appointed to the King's service on account of pre-eminence in their work. Being then questioned by them as to my reflections and they having opened the way into this broad field, the scribe spoke:

H · I suppose the use of letters is so old that it would be very difficult to find out who were the originators of them, although Pliny did name them.

E · It is said the Phoenicians were the first inventors of them and for this reason they were greatly renowned by the ancients. However, I should gladly hear your views about it.

G · I firmly believe that they were invented as early as necessity forced men to think about it – not in a single hour, not by a single individual, but gradually, since it is easy to add to things already invented. But this is not to my purpose, for I know well what you have written on the subject in your mastely Alphabet, having carefully drawn on the old authorities. It will satisfy me to learn from you the terms which you commonly use in your art of writing; and from you those you use in your printing.

H · Indeed, I am more than pleased to tell you, for knowing how careful you are to search out the proper uses of our French tongue, I long ago determined to give you some of its elements.

G · Tell me then the things which are most necessary in writing.

H · Pen, paper and ink.

G · What is required in the pen?

H · The first requirement is that it be well selected, then that it be well cut.

G · How should you select it?

H · From a quill that is long, clean, dry and little laden with fat.

G · How do you cut it?

H · The cutting is not the same for all, for those which have a soft and tender quill ought to be split but slightly and to have a very short nib. Those with a hard one ought to have a longer split and the nib made limber farther back, as this lengthening renders the pen less unruly in forming the letters well.

G · Is it a general rule that all pens must be split?

H · Not at all, since it is not always necessary to write delicately. Sometimes we are compelled to paint rather than write, as in making lettre de forme and gros bâtarde initials.

G · Then the pen-knife is one of your chief instruments, and, to put it neatly, is like your pens' schoolmaster since it so often loosens their tongue.

H · It is not the chief one, I believe – unless you wish to call chief the ruler, lead and compass, by which we guide our lines and control our writing.

G · So I will say one of the chief things, for I know that it is not essential if we compare it with the three major ones. Anyway

71 **Custodia** (Custodia Normal & Italic)

we are afraid that the writing will show through on the other side, we dab it with varnish. This we are generally forced to do when we are writing large letters.

G · Has the paper any part in making the letters appear more beautiful?

H · That rests merely with the whim of the writer. For some prefer to do their writing on highly finished paper, others on grey paper, others on blue paper, and still others on parchment or vellum.

G · And how should the ink be?

H · It ought to run well, and for this reason it should not be so thick as to be gummy. For the rest, it should be very black. These are the three things which we use most.

G · What method do you favour of teaching a child well?

H · The principal means is practice, and the care and diligence of the master, for one without the other accomplishes nothing.

G · What is practice? What is attained by it?

H · The child forms and steadies his hand, which is also another point extremely necessary for writing well. And if the pen is not so necessary that one cannot do without it, as in the old days when they used to write with the puncheon.

H · That was what they did before they had paper to use, and were forced to take the bark of trees.

G · It is still done in our time by those who have many affairs and who are much employed in various places. They have tablets on which they write with a fescue, to aid their memory.

H · Such writing ought not to be compared with the other.

G · Yes indeed, since it is useful. For all writing is good or worthwhile only according to the amount of service one gets from it to conduct ordinary affairs more ably. But let us pass on. What about the choice of paper?

H · What is most essential in the paper is that it should not 'drink' at all and that it be clean. Any that is otherwise is made for some other use rather than for writing, such as for making windows, book boards and for wrapping wares.

G · Yet you do make use of blotting paper.

H · We use it in place of pounce.

G · Is that all which is required of the paper?

H · Yes. Sometimes, however, when it is not well sized, so that

THIS IS NOT DONE, YOU SEE

73 Renard (Renard Titling)

this is not done, you see that a cramped and trembling hand is not able to do anything well, were it the best writer in the world.

G · Is it possible that practice alone so steadies the hand that it would be sufficient?

H · I mean practice guided by the master who, being careful, takes pains to train the child's hand, making him write sometimes on his knee, sometimes on a table, so as to make him steady and get him used to writing evenly under all conditions.

G · Then a master must be wonderfully careful!

H. If he is not so he is unworthy to bear the writing case or horn.

G · Then I do not wonder that there are so many botchers who occupy themselves only in erasing and scratching out what they do. But tell me about the examples.

H · In giving examples to children the good master should take heed that they serve as examples not only for writing well but also for learning to live well.

G · What should he do after this first point has been well observed?

H · He should proceed from the small to the great. He shows what is simple before showing the complex. He begins with the letters of the alphabet, demonstrating how to fashion well the form of each one of them.

G · Are the alphabets alike?

H · Not at all!

G · Then with which must he begin?

H · With the commonest and most used.

G · Which is the most used letter?

H · The commune courante, which is generally used in ordinary affairs.

G · What is he to do afterward?

H · If the parents want the children to go on, they can be taught the lettre carrée, the lettre ancienne, the lettre d'état, the lettre ronde, lettre de comptes, lettre de finances, la lettre Italique commune ou ronde ou d'exercice, la lettre Venecienne ronde ou carrée, the lettre pattée et droicte, the lettre de chevalerye and countless others made for pastime, like the panchée, gauche, couppée, renversée, frisée and those which one can invent at will and name according to their form.

G · After having shown the single letters, what do you do?

H · First we show how to make words of them, then afterward single lines, then two, three and four, then more and more accord–

ing to the capacity of the child.
G · How do you teach him to embellish letters and to paint well?
H · That is learned by the same method, i.e., by following the example given to the children. It is the case that they can by themselves learn how to make dashing strokes, after they are cunning in other matters and have a light touch.

Then those who naturally have a heavy

G · Well then, what are the principal parts of your art?

E · They are the types, the form or assemblage of them, and the press.

G · Is there anything else?

E · I am leaving out what we have in common with the writing master, like paper and ink – although our ink is not like theirs.

G · What is the difference?

E · The difference is that ours is made of turpentine, oil and lamp black. It is necessary that it should be thus.

G · Let us proceed then and begin with the types, since you have put them foremost. How are they made?

E · First the punch is made. This is a long piece of steel, on the end of which is engraved the desired character.

G · What becomes of that?

E · When it is done it is struck into copper and a matrix is made, which is nothing but the impression of the character struck, exactly as when a seal is impressed in wax.

G · What is the purpose of the character thus struck into copper?

E · Into this matrix the type metal, such as lead or tin, of which

G · Then those who naturally have a heavy hand are not likely to write well.

H · No. Nevertheless, practice can overcome this handicap in them.

G · The former are liable readily to grace their pens.

H · It is so.

G · It seems to me that you have now given enough about the methods to satisfy me with respect to writing.

It is to you I turn, E., since you offer to do me the favour of telling about this marvellous art of printing.

E · I do not wish to stop to speak of its excellence, knowing your appreciation of that is as good as I could make it. But as for the procedure which we follow, I will take it up gladly.

G · Then I shall question you in the same way as I have done with

H · and you will answer me, as I know you can.

E · That suits me.

they wish to make the type, is poured, in a mould.

G ◆ I understand what you mean. However, it seems to me very difficult to make that into types so expertly proportioned that they all go together exactly.

E · That is done by means of the mould, which is made of several pieces fastened together, by which all the types are made alike, being as they say of the same font.

G · The mould may thus take the matrix of an A as readily as that of a B and so on, and the A and B are therefore proportioned alike.

E · That is right.

G · It is made of several pieces, you say?

E · Yes, necessarily so, for otherwise the type would not be able to have those things necessary to it. First the mould is mounted on a block (the wood) against which there is a little bow which lifts. Then there is a plate, the long pieces (carriage) and the wire (nick) fastened to the long pieces. There are the blanks (body), the pins, the jets, the registers, the gallows (male gauge) and the striker (stool), all essential to the complete mould.

G · This, then, is how the fonts are cast inside the moulds, to which the matrices are attached. But how do you come to have so many kinds of types?

E · That is on account of the diversity of works that have to be printed, either in large or smaller letter. According to them the types have received different names.

G · Is it your opinion that, through being accustomed to make a book in a certain kind of type, they have called such type after it?

E · I understand it so, as in the composition of missals they called some missal types canon and petit canon de messel, glose de messel; lettre de Cicéro, lettre de S. Augustin, because they had been used to printing such authors with these types.

G · Where did the others get their names?

E · Some have taken them from nations which have used them commonly. Of this sort are some we call romain and gros romain or texte, ordinary romain, petit romain, and the italics, lettre françoise, and Greek type.

G · Have others been named for different reasons?

E · Oh yes. Because of their great beauty some are called mignonne, nonpareille and paragon. Others have taken their names elsewhere, such as gros and petit canon, texte, two line tourné letters, gros trait, grand and petit bourgeois, lettre batarde, lettre de somme or modern, and lettre de parchemin.

G · Are all these types made the same way?

E · Yes, and even the notes of music. It should be remarked that each kind of type has its capitals or versals, abbre-

81 Waver (Waver Bold Italic)

type has its capitals or versals, abbreviations, ligatures, numbers or figures, titling letters, accents, spaces, quadrats, divisions, distinctions.

G · But tell me, is everything printed at the press done from foundry material?

E · No. Sometimes they cut on wood lettres grises and flowered letters, fleurons, chapter headings and vignettes. And most of the portraits and figures which are put in a book, save those engraved on copper.

G · You have satisfied me on this point.

E · Tell me, if you please, about the form.

E · When it is a question of printing any book, it is given to the compositor, who assembles the types that are distributed separately in the case, in which there are as many boxes as there are different types.

G · I follow, so far.

E · Then he fastens the copy on which he wishes to work to a visorum, which is a long wooden piece that supports the copy, and for fear lest it become folded he fixes a mordant, which is a cleft stick going crosswise.

That done, he takes his composing stick, also of wood, wherein he sets the lines, and as he completes them he places them in a galley where the pages are made up.

G · Then do you print the pages, one after the other?

E · Not at all. But when he has set two or four or six or eight of them, depending on the size of the book, he imposes them all together in a chase. G. What is this chase?

E · It is a square made of six bars of iron of which four form the sides and the other two a cross at the middle, so that there are four small squares in which the pages are imposed.

G · Are all chases made this way?

E · No. Sometimes there is only one crosspiece and sometimes none at all. That is on account of the difference in the size of books.

G · These pages imposed, what does he do?

E · He justifies them and locks them with wooden furniture, of which some pieces are called headers (headsticks), tapered (side- and foot-) sticks, reglets and quota-

QUOTATIONS — SO CALLED BECAUSE

83 Nobel (Nobel Bold Condensed)

tions – so called because they are used for the quotations that are placed in the margins. G · That being done, how does he lock them in the chase? for

THERE MUST BE INNUMER- ABLE PIECES.

85 Ingo (Ingo Titling)

there must be innumerable pieces.

E · It is true. However, he locks them with quoins in such a way that all the pieces are pressed in from every side, like the staves of a wooden measure by its hoops.

G · I see how that is, for each one of the types is justified in proportion to every other one.

E · You are right.

G. And then afterward?

E · The form made up in this way is handed over to the two printers who operate the press.

G · It is necessary now for you to explain the press.

E · First, the press is made firm between two sister twins (cheeks), set upright on two paws (feet). They are joined by two summers (head and winter) and are made secure above with stays, pins and keys which hold fast and steady all the top part.

G · Then is it a business of such great force?

E · You will hear: Between the sister twins the screw (spindle) is located, fitted in the hose. The pivot (head) of this spindle enters into the nut supported by crampons.

It then rests on the stud bedded in the top of the platen. This platen is a large and broad piece of iron which covers all that has to be printed and is attached by means of rings.

G · This is not enough. What means is there to make the spindle go round?

E · There is a bar which, being pulled by the handle, lowers the spindle and, being pushed back on to its catch, raises it.

G · Then when work is under way the printer pulls the bar in order to bring the platen down on the form and when he wishes to take off his sheet he pushes the bar back.

E · It is so. But it must be understood that the form is put on a marble or stone set in the coffin, at the four corners of which there are corner irons holding the chase. This coffin is on a plank with cramp-irons underneath and runs backward and forward the length of the cradle (ribs) by means of a spit below, upon which the rounce is fitted.

G · Then turning the rounce brings all the coffin forward under the platen and sends it back again after the operation.

You are quite right. The cradle does

E · You are quite right. The cradle does not move, and is supported at one end by the press itself and at the other by a wooden upright called the foot (forestay). On the hind end of the coffin is the large (outer)

89 Sansa (Sansa Ultrablack Condensed)

the coffin is the large (outer) tympan, attached by means of iron joints, and the small (inner) tympan goes inside it, so that the blankets are held between them.

What are these blankets for? The blan-

91 Philips Script (Philips Script Bold)

G · What are these blankets for?

E · The blankets are placed between the platen and form lest the platen by its great hardness should batter it.

G · But is the paper never going to be laid on?

E · I am coming to that. The paper is laid on top of the tympan. It is pricked on to two small points fastened to the large tympan by means of screws and nuts, so it can be got at easily for the reiteration. The reiteration is done when the paper is turned over for printing on the other side.

G · The paper being stretched out thus, is it printed at once?

E · No, not yet, for it must be covered by a frisket, held firm by hasps.

G · What is this frisket?

E · It is a parchment covering all parts of the form not to be printed, such as the space between pages, the margins, and all white spaces.

G · It is done then, for all I can see.

E · Not yet, for it is necessary to have dampened the paper on the previous day so that it is evenly moist.

G · Why so?

E · Otherwise the ink, although very sticky, would not take hold. On being dampened the paper is placed between two planks so that it stays flat and takes the water better. Meanwhile the ink balls are being prepared.

G · What are the ink balls?

E · They are for putting ink on the form. They are made, first, of a wooden stock, then some well carded wool stuffed into it, which is covered by pelts nailed all round the wood. That done, ink is taken which clings to the leather and it is beaten on the form, which retains as much as is needed for printing.

G · Is it possible the type takes that without anything further:

E · It is, and for that reason the ink must be thick and sticky lest it should run while on the type.

G · What is there to do then?

E · The tympan is then lowered, the frisket being fixed, and taking the rounce by the handle the pressman makes the coffin enter halfway under the platen. The bar is pulled for the first time, the coffin is run on in the other half, and the bar pulled a second time.

G · Why is the coffin not run clear in the first time?

E · Because the platen cannot cover the whole form.

G · But what is there to do if it turns out that there is something wrong in the composition of the types?

E ✤ It is corrected after a proof of it has been seen. The form is unlocked with a shooting stick and hammer. Then the compositor pulls out the extra or faulty types with his bodkin and inserts others in their place. If there is a loose spot he fills in with quadrats or spaces or broken type. In short he can easily put in or take out as he likes.

G · That is an amazing thing!

E · While it is being done one of the printers adjusts the frisket and the other rubs out the ink with a brayer and spreads it with a slice so that it will be easier for the balls to take up.

G · I see that there are wonderful practices!

E · It is only the first sheet that costs so much, for after that they can be pulled one after another, two or three thousand or as many as are wanted.

G · And what is done with the form when all are printed?

E · When they are about to finish work they heat some lye in a kettle. This being done they put the form in a big trough where it is rubbed and cleansed with brush and lye, which gets rid of all the remaining ink. That done, they give it back again to the compositor for distribution of the types, each one to the box from which he had taken it.

G · I should never have thought there was so much to it! And I am very much pleased by the understanding you have given me by this discussion. However, I must see it actually done, if you please. I have, moreover, something to get printed.

E · We will do it whenever you wish. Also you will be introduced to many things which I have perhaps overlooked. But it is getting late. Let us go into the city.

LET US GO INTO THE CITY.

Commentary on the typefaces

Short descriptions of my typefaces and fonts follow. This list is not really complete: some projects have simply been lost, others have been lost due to superseded technology, some were purely industrial in application and may now have a life of their own. All this follows from the nature of type design, which is often simply jobbing work. But this is the fullest list I can make at this stage.

Arnhem The Werkplaats Typografie in Arnhem was approached to do a redesign for the *Nederlandse Staatscourant*, the daily newspaper of the Dutch state. One of the teachers there, Karel Martens, asked if I would be interested in saying something about the choice of a newspaper typefaces. This was late 1998. In the end, the whole adventure ended up with a custom-made typeface for the *Staatscourant*; though for internal political reasons they never used it. Arnhem has a roman, an italic and matching small caps in four weights. As well as that it has two weights of 'Fine' variants in roman and italic. When it was in a finished enough state, it began to be used by friends who knew about the typeface, for example in Hyphen Press books, by Carl-H.K. Zakrisson for the new Danish hymn book, and by the Dutch design group Die Twee. Arnhem was released by OurType at the end of 2002.

Boekblad *Boekblad*, the trade magazine for the book world in the Netherlands, wanted to have a more colourful and fresher look. Our Quadraat group proposed the Quadraat typeface for the text, and a good display typeface was needed. I made some characters for display just for fun, which we inserted among other proposals. To my surprise these were then taken rather seriously, resulting in my first custom-made typeface. This was done in 1993.

Brand A sanserif family in normal and bold, roman and italic, all with matching condensed variants. A project done to investigate how much room there is still in the sector of Verdana-like office fonts, and with a slightly more elegant, humane and friendlier tone of voice. Enhanced for low-resolution screen representation. Not yet released.

Custodia A single-weight roman, italic and matching small caps, with a seventeenth-century flavour. It was made in 2002 for good friends who specialize in designing books, and was originally meant for use in the Custodia Foundation publications.

Denda A contemporary sanserif initiated in 2000 by TBWA\Designers Company for their redesign of Canon Europe packaging. This typeface comes in four weights, in roman and in matching italics: for use by Canon Europe in general publicity, manuals, and packaging. It is a custom-made design, not publicly available.

Fresco A large family that — unlike Quadraat, which evolved gradually over the years — was planned from the outset. The family consists of serif and matching sanserif variants. The sans also has a playful slab-serif variant, while the serif has a casual variant. The sans and the serif have matching script variants. Those fonts that will be used for book-work also have small-capital variants. The family comes in five weights, with condensed versions, lining figures, non-lining figures, and x-height lining figures. Its character can be described as a refreshment of traditional and conventional issues: it is definitely a contemporary typeface, shamelessly embracing all the good given by tradition. Fresco was first shown in October 1998 in the Dutch design magazine *Items*. The first Fresco fonts were released by OurType early in 2003.

Ingo Another typeface that followed from a request by designer friends. It had to be something based on classical proportions, but not dusty; maybe even a bit stubborn or strange, but never crossing the line of acceptance. It had to have display qualities but also be suitable for normal text setting. To my surprise it was used on a billboard campaign for Dutch ING Bank (2001).

Lambrusco This was done in 1995, essentially for educational purposes. It is a letter constructed with mathematical forms only. Before this book, it had been seen only once in print: the 1996 *Typocalender* produced by the printers Rosbeek, for which each month's display was in the hands of a different Dutch designer.

Monitor A sanserif roman and italic in two weights, especially for office use, made in 2001.

Nobel (designed with Andrea Fuchs) Some time in 1993, Andrea Fuchs, then a student graphic designer at the Arnhem school of art, approached me saying that there was a typeface called Nobel in the letterpress workshop there, but that this type was not available on the school's computers. The message had a spark of despair. After a short explanation and the suggestion of some possible solutions, Andrea decided to do the job herself. Convinced by her determination, I decided to give a helping hand. Nobel, a revival of the Dutch version of the Berlin Grotesk produced by Tetterode in the late-1920s is a complete family. It was released by the Dutch Type Foundry in 1995.

Oce_L_EA A two-weight roman (normal and bold) in Extended Latin A, especially designed for use in the interfaces of a number of Océ's products, working together with Océ Symbols. This was done in 2002. (Not shown.)

Philips Cellesse A logo designed for the anti-cellulitis apparatus called Cellesse was the start of a whole family of logos designed for personal care products, all strongly related to each other. After a while I decided to create an entire font so that future logos could simply be typed in. (1995-8; see page 136.)

Philips MPH font In 2000 I was asked by Philips to design a rather condensed typeface for DVD interfaces. After some trials we found an acceptable width, allowing enough words to fit into a line and still be readable. This had to be done in a special character set known by the industry as MPH, hence the name. The family consists of two widths: narrow and extremely narrow. (See page 118.)

Philips screen font family A grotesque-like family of four fonts based on early bitmap fonts that I had made for Philips. In 1994 I built outlines around these bitmaps — outlines which could be hinted. Jelle Bosma did this hinting. (Not shown.)

Philips Script Used to create a more coherent lettering on kitchen utensils produced by Philips. It had to be script-like, spontaneous, casual, with a contemporary atmosphere and not too arts-and-crafty. The script has three weights, some extra ligatures, but avoids connected letters. Produced for Philips in 1997.

Quadraat My first commercially available type design, which grew to a large family, with serif, sanserif, small capitals, display and headline fonts, as well as monospaced variants. The seriffed fonts have a matching Cyrillic. The family was developed from the early 1990s through to 1998. This development and expansion of Quadraat owes much to changes in the typographic landscape over the last decade. Originally it was meant for bookish productions only, but requests from various designer friends led me to design a matching sans, and the rest followed. The family was and is used widely for all kinds of purposes.

Renard From 1987 I was a frequent visitor to the Plantin-Moretus archives in Antwerp. The book *Counterpunch* was one outcome of these visits, the Renard typeface was another. It is a revival of Hendrik van den Keere's 2-line Double Pica Roman, cut around 1570. So Renard is a true Flemish Garamond: stout in character and historically the opening for the forms of the 'Dutch' roman ('le goût hollandais'). The typeface was shown for the first time in a leaflet announcing *Counterpunch*, distributed at the ATypI conference of 1993, held in Antwerp. Renard was released by The Enschedé Fount Foundry in 1998. It has three weights of roman and italic, with matching small caps. The specimen here shows its so far unreleased titling fonts.

Romanée (designed with Peter Matthias Noordzij) The book *Adieu aesthetica & mooie pagina's* was published to accompany the exhibition 'J. van Krimpen en het "schoone boek"' held in The Hague in 1995. Martin Majoor was the designer of this book and knew that there were plans for a digital Romanée. So he asked Matthias Noordzij if there was an acceptable digital version. At that time there was not. So then we rolled up our sleeves and got the typeface done for that book.

Sansa A sanserif that benefits from the liberties taken in recent sanserif design, without overdoing them, yet retaining much character. There are no small caps or non-lining figures. So it is definitely non-bookish, but is still an effective type for a wide range of daily uses. It has four weights of roman and italic, and has the same in the matching condensed family. The condensed has an ultra black weight in roman and italic. Sansa was released by OurType at the end of 2002.

Sloane This is a formal script-like design based on examples that date from the late seventeenth century. This is a personal exercise in creating four different flavours, just by making small changes to one master, ranging from formal to informal. Now with the OpenType format there are more possibilities for the actual use of designs like this. Sloane was done in 1996. Not yet released.

Switchblade For a time I felt the need to decorate my work-room with texts composed in my own stencil designs (see, for example, the one reproduced on page 108). Some years later, in 1995, these pieces caught my attention again and some of them I translated into digital type. The one shown here has not had much thought given to its name, but it's clear that this name refers to the knife-blade-like letter elements. Things like this are done for the sheer fun of it. OurType plans a release for a little display family consisting of some of these designs.

Waver Waver came into existence in 1997, during my last days at Het Lab. One of our commissioners wanted some packaging to be done. Erik Vos and I decided that we needed brisk lettering. I had to come up with something catchy and I think I did. With some distance now, it's clear that this font was inspired by a display typeface I always liked very much, and which was used effectively on the covers of the Zephyr paperbacks of the 1940s. I mean, of course, the Allegro typeface. Not yet released.

In colour

The selection of work shown in this section has been made to give a representative picture. We have chosen things that need to be seen in colour: a type designer's activity need not be entirely black and white, nor need it be confined to type. Many of the pieces here make use of lettering in the broadest sense. For captions on these pieces, see page 121. Dimensions are given in centimetres, height followed by width.

punkafe fumeurs is na de uk subs tot vier uur open!

Quidquid

præcipies

esto

brevis .

Tutta combotto
é composto di
opposizioni...
Impara à vedere
le cose indietro
revolta osotto
sopra.

All behavior consists of opposites...
learn to see things backwards,
inside out, and upside down.

god sends meat
the devil sends cooks

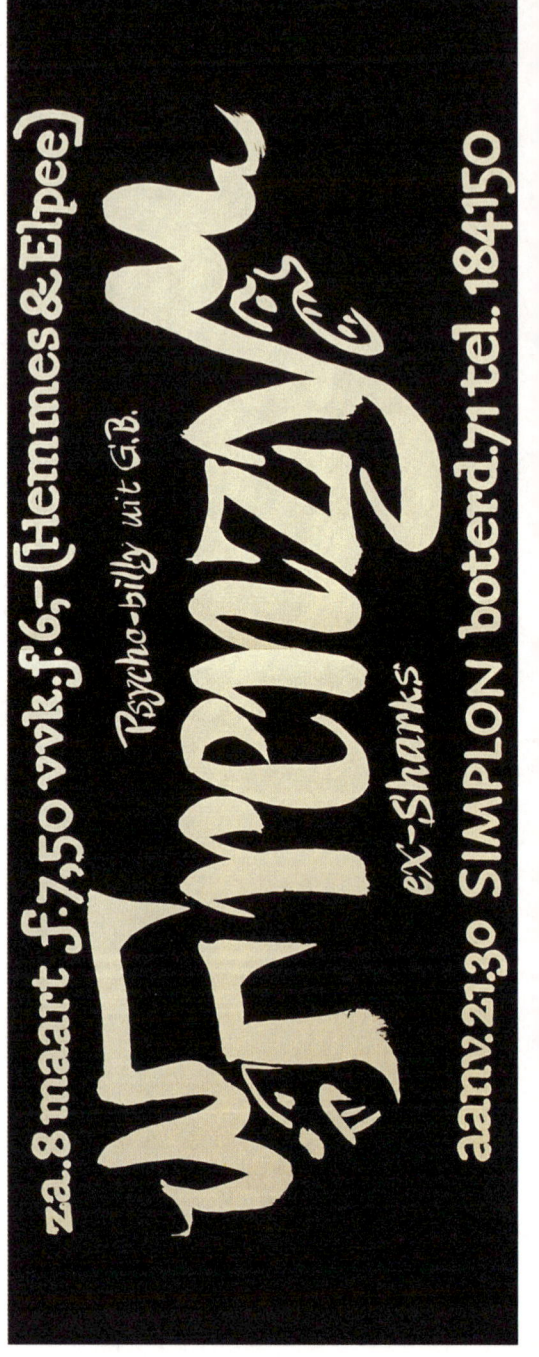

ABCDEF
123456789
abcdefghi
.,.;?!-¿¡—(

ABCDEF
123456789
abcdefghij
.,.;?!-¿¡—(

minimum minder dan van overheid

de kamer waar ilja iljitsj lag, leek op het eerste gezicht
met zorg gemeubileerd. er stond een bureau van mahonie
er prijken twee met zijde beklede sofa's, enige fraaie kam
schermen, waarop vogels en vruchten waren geborduurd,
de natuur niet voorkomen. er waren zijden gordijnen en ta

imum minder dan overheid

amer waar ilja iljitsj lag leek op het eerste gez
t zorg gemeubileerd. er stond een bureau van m
rijken twee met zijde beklede sofa's, enige fra
ermen, waarop vogels en vruchten waren gebor
natuur niet voorkomen. er waren zijden gordijne

e kamer waar ilja iljitsj lag, leek op het eerste gezicht
et zorg gemeubileerd. er stond een bureau van maho
r prijken twee met zijde beklede sofa s, enige fraaie ka
chermen, waarop vogels en vruchten waren geborduu
e natuur niet voorkomen, er waren zijden gordijnen en
childenjen, bronzen beeldjes, porselein en talloze mod
nuistenjen.

32	BLUE	20	2	A PIN 12
34	YELLOW	20	27½	C TO K
35	RED	16	25½	D TO K
36	YELLOW	20	30½	G TO K
14	BLUE	18	25½	TO K
49	WHITE	20	17½	M TO N
55	RED	20	11½	F TO A PIN 11

Maria
Eén van de
del Mar
grootste vertolkers
Bonet
van het Catalaanse lied.

VREDENBURG UTRECHT

ZONDAG 7 MEI – 20.15 UUR
ƒ 20,–/INFORMATIE 030-31 31 44

■ **'La Cambiale di Matrimonio'**
farsa giocosa in un atto ■ Gioachino Rossini ■
muzikale leiding: Lawrence Renes ■ regie: Javier López Piñón
■ solisten: Marcel Boone, Francien van der Heijden/Renate Arends, Martin van Os/
Otto Bouwknegt, Anton Saris, Maarten van Maanen, Sheila van Rheenen/Esther Been

■ **'The Bear'** an extravaganza in one act ■
Sir William Walton ■ muzikale leiding: Kenneth Montgomery,
■ regie: Carl van der Plas ■ solisten: Susan Glanzberg, Romain Bischoff,
René Swankhuizen ■ twee eenacters door studenten van de
OPERAKLAS [in samenwerking met het Utrechts Conservatorium] ■ uitvoeringen: 10, 13, 15 en 17 december,
20.00 uur Koninklijk Conservatorium,
Kees van Baarenzaal ■ Juliana van Stolberglaan 1, Den Haag.
Ticketshop: (070) 381 42 51 ■ toegangsprijs ƒ10,–

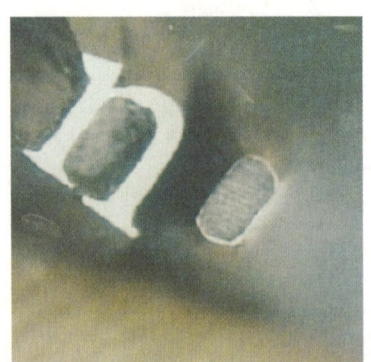
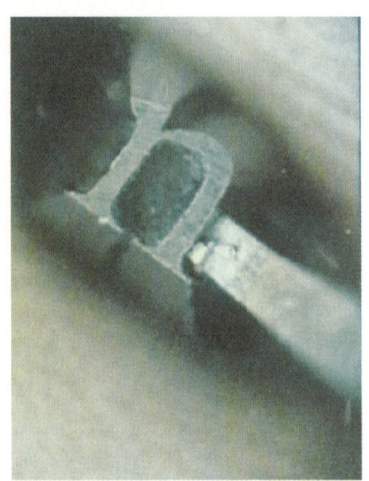
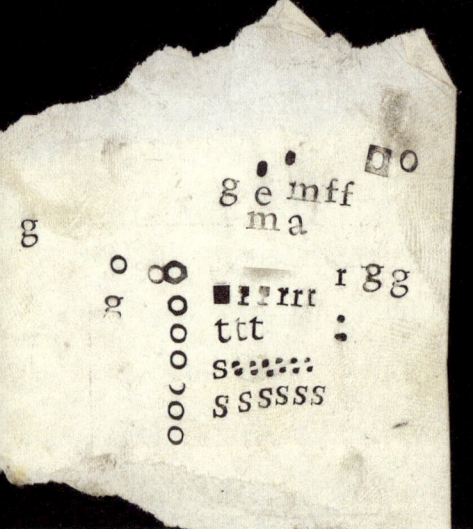

Drie uitvergrotingen van een originele stempel van de Gras Canon Romain en een afdruk op ware grootte

Hendrik van den Keere:
Gras Canon Romain

*1540
†1580
±1572

Renard italic two 80 p
Renard two 80 p

Renard regular
Renard italic
Renard small capitals

RENARD

Titling capitals 97 p

Renard two 12 p

Dit blad is een kennismaking met de Renard, een eigentijdse Garamond met het accent op karakter.

De Gras Canon Romain van de Vlaamse stempelsnijder Hendrik van den Keere, waarop de onderkast van de Renard is gebaseerd, geeft een beeld dat men in eerste instantie niet associeert met de klassieke chique Garamond-snit. Bovendien is deze romein wat vreemd van proportie. De verhoudingen van de letters onderling lijken iets uit balans te zijn en het gewicht is ronduit zwaar, zoals te zien is in onderstaande illustraties. Dit zijn vermoedelijk de redenen geweest waarom men tot nu toe aan deze letter is voorbijgegaan. Het zijn evenwel juist deze eigenaardigheden die interessant zijn. En die ik zeker niet bestempel als 'fout', iets wat anderen –en zeker als men kijkt met de ogen van een letterontwerper- in eerste instantie geneigd zijn te doen. ¶ Stempels van letters zijn niet zozeer letters maar veeleer kleine sculpturen van letters. Tijdens het stempelsnijden wordt het beeld van de letter als het ware bevrijd door het teveel aan materie weg te halen. Dat wat eenmaal is weggehaald kan niet meer worden toegevoegd. De beslissingen die de stempelsnijder maakt om het beeld van de stempel te veranderen zijn bindend. Dit klinkt onaantrekkelijk en dat zal het zeker ook zijn voor een onervaren persoon; het is echter reuze spannend voor degenen die bekend en ervaren zijn met het proces. Juist in dit spanningsveld van twijfel -wel of niet veranderen- vinden zij vaak de persoonlijke uitdaging en voldoening. ¶ Het is ook in dit mistig gebied waarin door allerlei vakmensen beslissingen wel intuïtief worden genomen. Dit resulteert vaak in ontwerpen van een charme en karakter dat moeilijk onder woorden is te brengen. Vandaar ook de naam Renard. Naast het feit dat deze bekende fabel *'van den vos Reynarde'* afkomstig is uit Vlaamse contreien, is de vos synoniem voor de combinatie van ervaring, lef en intuïtie.

Fred Smeijers, september 1997

Met dank aan: Museum Plantin-Moretus – Antwerpen, Het Lab grafisch ontwerpers – Arnhem. Bijlage bij Hollandse hoogte 23/24 (1997).

Fred Smeijers
Enschedé Font
Foundry © 1997
The Netherlands

Philishave

Ladyshave

Navigatie

Naam	Duur	Datum	Programma	Zien	Hervat	Wisse
OTR	0:19:41	23/Sep	NED3	●	●	●
OTR	1:01:51	17/Sep	NED2	●	●	●
APPLE	0:29:28	15/Sep	NED3	●	●	●
OTR	0:04:52	11/Sep	CANU	●	●	●
HERGE	1:14:39	02/Sep	CANU	●	●	●

Titels Totaal 15   1/3 pagina
Tijd verschuiving

```
Selecteren      : ▲▼◄►    Afspelen         : PLAY
Verlaten        : RETURN   Vooruitblik      : OK
Vorige Pagina   : ◄◄       Volgende Pagina  : ►►
Voer Naam In    : TITLE
```

Timer Programmering

Start Tijd	21 : 07
Eind Tijd	22 : 37
Datum	Wo. / 24/Sep
Programma	P20/280MHz
Frequencie	Eenmalig
Aflevering	1
Opn. Mode	SQ
VPS/PDC	Uit

Opslaan

Naam :

```
Selecteren : ▲▼◄►
Kiezen     : OK
Verlaten   : RETURN
```

ShowView No.

```
Cijfers     : 0 - 9
Verplaatsen : ◄►
Wissen      : CLEAR
Kiezen      : OK
Verlaten    : RETURN
```

QUOTE

page 105
'Punkafe' poster (100 x 70). A stencil poster made during my time at the Simplon youth centre in Groningen, 1985-6. I cut a stencil alphabet in film, then someone else did the stencilling with a waterproof marker.

106
A writing exercise done at Groningen, shown here at real size. This is a formal italic written with a broad pen; the 'ink' was diluted photo-opaque.

107
Two writing exercises done on my own initiative as a student at Arnhem. The example at the top ('Tutta') is a rotunda — done with a broad pen. The lower piece ('All behavior') was written with a slightly flexible broad-nibbed quill, following no particular historical style. Both are shown here at 90 per cent of real size.

108
Two pieces from my time at the Simplon youth centre in Groningen, 1985-6. The lettering for the 'Frenzy' silk-screen poster was painted with a brush directly onto the screen with sugar solution. The writing exercise (19 x 54) was done with colour pencils using stencil letters. The colours are arbitrarily distributed here, to make it a more playful thing, though in other pieces of the time I used colour to show the construction of the written letters.

109
Above: a pair of copper cuff-links that I made for Martin Majoor in the 1980s. The letters were written with a pen on soft etching ground, then carefully etched in. The Kevin Coyne poster (50 x 65), also for the Simplon, was printed silk-screen. I cut the lettering with a scalpel in film.

110
A typical piece from my time with Océ, often working there together with Martin Majoor. Océ had bought outline Times Roman fonts from Bitstream, which were then rasterized by their machines to give bitmaps. The sample above is the raw output. Below, some output after Martin and I had made adjustments.

page 111
Above: Grey-scaled screen fonts designed for Océ in 1988. First, hand-adjusted bitmaps without grey-scaling; then with grey-scales generated automatically from outlines; third — the final grey-scaled font, with hand-adjusted bitmaps. Note the dramatic improvement in the 'm' ('gemeubileerd'), which simply does not work in the version without grey-scaling. In the final font the words (including the counters) sit in a box of grey, while the word space is 100 per cent light and so shines out.
Below: Océ made a printer for microfiches carrying technical drawings. A code for each drawing was superimposed on the image, and had to be visible no matter what was drawn underneath. The engineers had assumed that these letters should be neutral and monoline, like the DIN alphabet. My solution was to make much fatter letters with slab-serifs, but also transparent: pixel on, pixel off.

112
A silk-screen poster for the Vredenburg music centre (111.5 x 38).
The lettering, done by hand, was an early trial for the kind of letterforms used in the Quadraat italic.

113
One of the silk-screen posters (80 x 80) that I designed for the Royal Conservatory in The Hague, using text set in the Quadraat typeface. Photographed in the Quadraat studio in Arnhem; the bicycle belonged to Evert Bloemsma.

114
At the top, two photos from a TV screen during one of my punchcutting demonstrations: a graver cutting an 'n', and an 'n' with the top of a counterpunch.
Then, in the second row, two smoke-proofs are shown. On the left is a set of real smoke-proofs, shown at real size. On the right, an explanatory enlarged scan of smoke-proofs made at the TypeLab meeting that Petr van Blokland and others held in Paris, 1993. In a fit of digital madness typical of that time, shadows were added to the images.
Below is the cover of *Counterpunch*, with the rear flap folded out. On the flaps of the book we reproduced the Académie Royale's engravings of the typefounding process.

page 115
The specimen of Renard (30 x 42) made to accompany the article I wrote on the typeface for *Hollandse Hoogte* (no. 23-24, 1997): it was inserted loose in the magazine. Printed by Jan de Jong, Amsterdam, on very thin paper.

116
This was the poster (60 x 42) for the Jan Van Krimpen exhibition held at the Meermanno Museum in 1995. The chief difficulty here was that none of Van Krimpen's own typefaces, as currently available, were really suitable for use in display sizes. So I used Bram de Does's Lexicon, which is certainly also part of the Van Krimpen's Dutch tradition. The pictures of his work in the margins were taken from the material of the accompanying book, *Adieu aesthetica & mooie pagina's!*, which Martin Majoor designed.

117
After some screen fonts work for Philips, Dingeman Kuilman asked me to work on their Philishave logo. This led to other logos for Philips products, as part of a more coherent graphic identity for the company. The Philishave logo applied on the football field: France-Italy in the Euro 2000 final.
Below: The illustration shows the proposal I made with Erik Vos of Het Lab for the letters on the roof of the new Amsterdam bus station, due for completion in 2009. It will stand between the main railway station and the river. The commissioner is the Gemeente Amsterdam (Dienst Infrastructuur en Vervoer); the architects are Benthem Crouwel, Amsterdam.

118
The screen pictures here show my fonts for this Philips DVD apparatus.

119
This page shows some of my commercial lettering from recent years. In the top row: *Quote* is a magazine for business people; this is my masthead for it. The work was commissioned by TBWA\Campaign Company, Amsterdam.
 The Philips video box uses my lettering in the HG logo. The development of the letters and the rest of the box were done by other designers.
In the second row, the Friesche Vlag packet shows the script lettering that I designed for these packs. The commissioner was BrandNew Design, Weesp. Finally, one of a set of soup packets. Here again I designed just the lettering, with the rest of the pack done by others. For this 'blackboard writing', I painted

some cardboard with blackboard paint and worked on that. The commissioner was VBAT, Schiphol.

page 120
At the top are the first two printed specimens for the OurType label with FontShop Benelux, designed by Corina Cotorobai in 2003. These have A3 pages (folding to A4), and a newspaper feel to them.
Below, a picture from the stencil research project with Eric Kindel at the University of Reading. We see some letters stencilled by Eric, with an example of the stencils I cut.

FS (right) with Martin Majoor (left) in Groningen, 1985. Behind them is the 'typographers' hospital'.

Year by year

The work I do has to relate strongly to the things that I love and respect. If you have to work eight hours a day on something that you do not like or in which you are not interested, that's a crime. I never liked being bored and I hardly ever was, neither as a child nor as an adult. But school was a problem for me. This was and still is a very inefficient system, and it cut me off from my personal interests, taking away big chunks of valuable time. I was a critical pupil, but never nasty.
I respected the teachers too much for that. And although most of them came up with things that could not really interest me, I found no fun in being a nuisance. By then I had already learned to be patient. So I had good relations with most of the teachers, and my low marks did not affect these relations. There were some subjects that interested me — drawing, physics, biology, history — and in these I excelled. School is a stupid system. It deals with children as a mass, rather than with the individual. Since maths could not interest me, it blocked off any future in a technical direction. That did not bother me at all, since school was a temporary thing and not of any influence on my life, or so I thought. So, as soon as possible, I left. A simple job was better than school. My dad, who recognized the mistake, nevertheless arranged a dull job for me. He said 'if you want to leave school, then you should have a proper job'. I ended up behind an assembly belt. But I went back to school in no time, just as my father had planned.
I decided that two more years of school would enable me to apply to an art academy, and that would be a far better thing than the assembly belt with its narrowly defined horizons. So, by taking school even less seriously than I already had done, it became easier. After the two years I got my final diploma and applied for three schools of art. I was accepted by all three of them, and chose Arnhem — I suppose because it was the one furthest from home. At that point I was planning a career as an illustrator. From the age of fifteen, I had already had some contacts with professional illustrators. Commercial illustrations, but also more conventional work, such as educational or real book illustrations, were what caught my attention.

‖ **1980** Arnhem changed some things. I met good allies and teachers there. Alexander Verberne was probably the most influential of them. Further, there was Karel Martens and Jan Vermeulen. All of them were typographers in the true sense of the word, or perhaps typographer / graphic designer in the case of Karel. However Alexander Verberne's writing classes were what I loved most, followed by his lettering classes in the second year. Meanwhile Martin Majoor and I had become good friends, and for some years we shared rooms in the same house. This was a good thing. We stimulated each other much, and we became part of a circle of interested student friends, among them Wim Westerveld and Wigger Bierma. All this created a very enthusiastic climate among the students themselves — something that is extremely valuable.
Jan Vermeulen focused on type and its history, the use of it, and the differences between typefaces, while Verberne was the one who let us write and draw letters and type ourselves. With the sudden departure of Jan Vermeulen a gap had to be filled, and Nico Spelbrink of BRS in Amsterdam came to give us some guest lessons. Looking at the proposals that we had made for an italic alphabet, in Alexander's classes, he asked if we would be interested in justifying them on a unit system. So we did that, and this imaginary production process made it possible for us to look at our own letters in relation to typographic measurements. And that enabled us to produce sample texts in our type exactly to 10 point size, and compare its performance with real typefaces.

‖ **1983** Gerrit Noordzij had started the idea for a Lecturis publication on student proposals for new type designs and asked his friend Alexander Verberne if he had anything to contribute. Alexander proposed us, and so we ended up in this publication.
Another eye-catching publication that we took part in was a typography project with Karel Martens and Stephan Saaltink.
It consisted of interviews with ten active designers, and we had to edit the texts ourselves and make a proper publication of the interview. Everything was actually printed — still rare those days — by sponsoring printers, and the ten booklets were brought together in a box. This was well received by the trade press. Martin's booklet on Harry Sierman was regarded as the most perfect, and mine (on Martin van Duynhoven) was considered the most original.

The type group gradually became smaller. Most students turned their thoughts to general design work – after all that is what they had come for. But they were also forced to do this, because some of the teachers thought it unwise to devote too much time to studying type. Martin started to make photographs and spent more time on illustration. I became involved in the publication of subcultural items, especially posters for all kinds of bands, usually silk-screen printed. Meanwhile we kept our interest in type design alive, as much as time let us. I remember buying an old reproduction camera so that we could make reductions of our designs outside the Academy. Also we had bought an old Staromat display photosetter, and made our own type-strips in the Noordzij way.

|| **1985** This was also the time when I had to worry about doing 'national service' in the armed forces. There was no way in which I would do that, so I applied to opt out for reasons of conscience. After my application was accepted, I had to find a position doing socially useful work, or else such a place would be found for you. Soon I had found a good place in Groningen, in the north of the country. It was a youth centre called Simplon, and my duty was to design and print all the necessary publicity for the activities there, such as music gigs, cinema, the bar and café, and so on. I had volunteers and material at my disposal. There was a silk-screen workshop, a darkroom with a reproduction camera, a design room, an A4 offset press, an IBM golfball typewriter, and a video workshop. They were intense days, in which I could apply all the experience I had already acquired and explore much more. After a year we were allowed to start a computer workshop, using the then popular BBC computers. These computers could be connected to a video camera. By this means I started to digitize – to scan, so to speak – my own designs. There was also a pixel drawing program in which I improved these images. Then you could put them into a kind of font and compose text, which could be printed on a dot-matrix printer. It was a primitive way of creating digital type.

Martin and Wim had in the meantime done some work at URW in Hamburg. There they created outlines of their student work. (Outlines were invented in Hamburg and not in Silicon Valley.) Of course we exchanged information. Wim went to Amsterdam to work for Nico Spelbrink, our mutual guest teacher, and Jeanne de Bont of Océ had met Martin and offered him a job there. Océ was and is a Dutch diazo and copier manufacturer which had developed its own mid-volume laser printer. But typography was a new discipline for them, so they needed skill and knowledge in matters of type. I had first to finish my time in Groningen. When that was done, I could do some custom work for BRS and spend some time with Wim in Amsterdam, until the moment when Martin and Jeanne needed help with all the work they had at Océ.

|| **1987** At Océ Martin and I were reunited. The fact that we both had a proper job meant that we had some money to spend. We travelled every year to London in search of out-of-print books on typography, often quite successfully. Books such as Oliver Simon's *Introduction to typography* or Geoffrey Dowding's *Factors in the choice of typefaces* were welcome titles. And at Océ there was enough to do: many battles to be fought, much to be researched and experimented with. These were exciting days too in the larger world of typography. We kept informed by reading *The Seybold Report*, which Océ subscribed to. We were facing the problems of the early days of rasterization of outlines, without any hinting. Then there was the fact that the Océ printers were white writers rather than black writers. Besides the rasterization mistakes, we had also to fatten the characters, so that they did not appear broken on the printed page. At first these were all bitmap fonts, so every size meant an entire font to be made. We also dealt with on-screen representation and 'wysiwyg' problems. All this gave us buckets of work and lots of things to consider. We had constant contact with the Océ technicians, and this did not always go smoothly. The two disciplines of engineering and design had to get used to each other. Then it was Martin's turn to face the national service problem and he had to leave, following the path that I had gone down. He worked in Utrecht at the Vredenburg music centre, doing their publicity together with the in-house designer Jan Willem den Hartog. At Océ, together with Jeanne de Bont and Henk Lamers, we had to find ways to speed things up and make them more efficient. As well as research and some production work, I had to train new people, keeping an eye on quality and defining standards. Further, I had to spend more time with technicians and create more mutual respect. It was their questions that turned me to punchcutting. I made frequent visits to

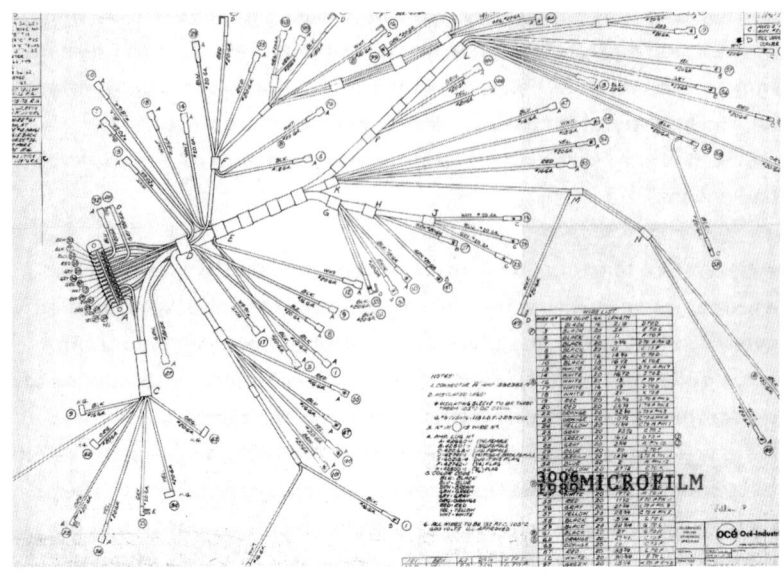

The whole of a sheet from the Océ microfiche printer. For a detail showing the fonts for this device, see page 111.

the Plantin-Moretus Museum in Antwerp and, although I did not know it then, the foundations of my book *Counterpunch* began to be laid.

By now the Macintosh culture was well on its way, and next to our Sun machines running Bitstream's Toolbox (one of the many versions), we turned to the Macintosh and to pioneer programs such as Mac-Ikarus, written by Petr van Blokland. In my spare time I experimented a good deal, and although Martin was at the Vredenburg, we had close contact. It was at that time that Martin started to work on his Scala typeface, which was designed in the first place for the Vredenburg publicity.

Meanwhile Just van Rossum and Peter Verheul did an internship at Océ. As well as their proper work, they had plenty of experiments going on, and I remember Just bringing along one of the first Fontographer versions.

I was asked to do some teaching at my old school, the Academy in Arnhem. Jantien Bos, the head of graphic design, wanted someone who understood the effects of digital media on type and typography. Although this was not allowed by Océ, I just went ahead did it. Each week I took up one day of holiday leave and spent that on teaching in Arnhem. After all my holiday allowance had been used up, Océ had to accept me doing this, or else I would simply quit the firm. A great help here was the design manager, Dries Vermeulen, who had come to understand that only a permissive attitude could keep my enthusiasm focused on Océ's interests.

|| **1991** My work at Océ went on for some years. But in my fifth year of clocking-in, the company was in some state of crisis. Profits were not what the directors wanted them to be, and the R & D department was responsible for these losses. The atmosphere of the whole place was grey – even greyer than that it already had been. Soon it was filled only with moody engineers who were scared to lose their jobs. Our department had to face big cuts. So I decided to help the firm by leaving, although they had rather I stayed, and were intending for some other people to go. Anyway, I just went. I needed some new horizons. As well as teaching in Arnhem, I did some book-production work together with an old friend, Wigger Bierma. Then in January 1991 Robin Kinross came from London, on the advice of Fransje Berserik, to visit Martin Majoor in Arnhem. I was still in Venlo, in the south of the

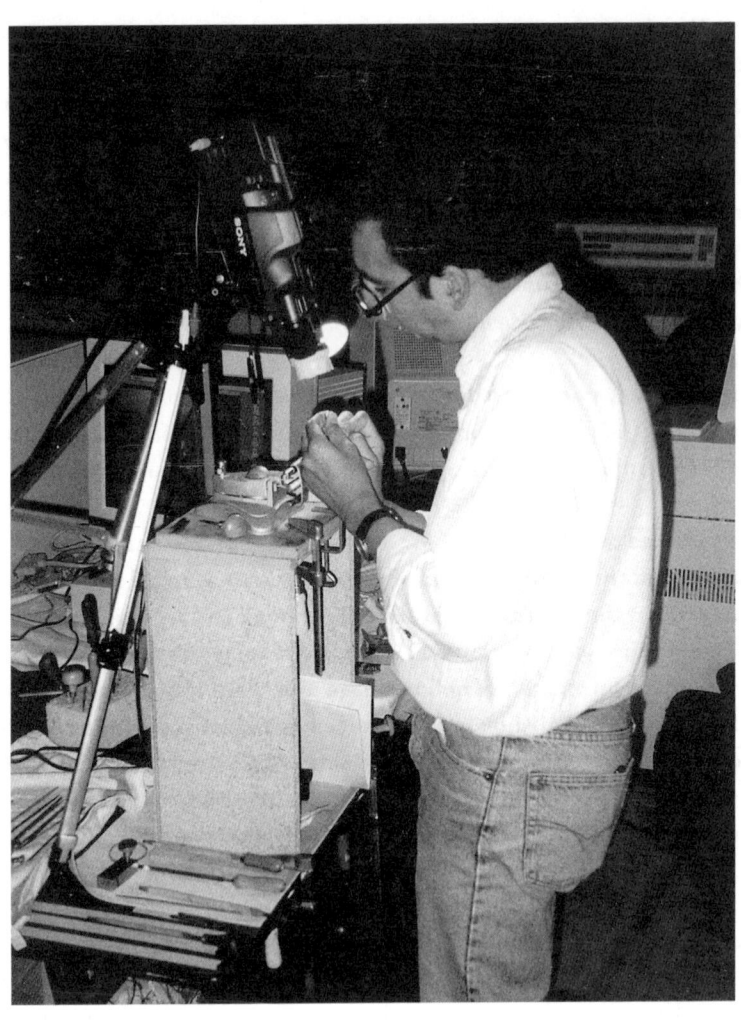

A punchcutting demonstration, held in my work room at Arnhem, 1990s.

Netherlands, but Martin asked me to come up and bring some work. And in that conversation with Robin the idea of writing a book about my work in punchcutting first crystallized. Soon after this visit I moved back to live in Arnhem, and with two other designers – Jan Willem den Hartog and Jan Erik Fokke – I started the graphic design group Quadraat. Later on we were joined by Josée Langen and Peter Paul Kloosterman.

‖ **1992** In the first year of our practice's existence I finished the typeface I had been working on. We changed its name from Amano to Quadraat, after the name of design group. Martin had his office upstairs in the same building, so again there was close contact with him, especially in anything to do with type.

Our contacts with Just van Rossum and Erik van Blokland led to Erik Spiekermann, and so to FontShop. Scala was now finished, and it became one of the first releases on the FontShop's FontFont label. Quadraat followed it, announced by a small specimen designed and produced in Arnhem, and partly sponsored by FontShop International. In September, Martin and I went to the ATypI meeting in Budapest, and I began to distribute the Quadraat specimen. I met Robin again there too, and we talked more about this book on the punchcutting. So, back from Budapest, I started to collect the notes and texts I had already written, and the illustrations I had drawn. It seemed too little, so a long period of expansion started – constantly interrupted by daily work and other projects. I had also started to work on a revival of one of Hendrik van den Keere's typefaces, which was taken on by The Enschedé Font Foundry.

‖ **1993** ATypI was held in Antwerp, and for this meeting we made a leaflet announcing *Counterpunch*. For the text we used the Van den Keere typeface for the first time – now given the name Renard. Further, I gave my first punchcutting demonstration at the TypeLab meeting that was held in Paris. I had bought a second-hand video camera which I connected to a television. I attached an extra lens to the video camera's lens and this enabled me to make really large magnifications. These images were sent directly to the TV screen, so that people could clearly see what I was doing when cutting a 12 point punch.

Another job in 1995 was the digitization of Van Krimpen's Romanée. Here I am surrounded by materials for the project. See page 116 for the poster I designed for the Van Krimpen exhibition of that year.

‖ **1994** Martin asked me for some advice and help with the production of his Telefont typeface. He had landed this commission as part of his redesign of the Dutch telephone books. I made the first trial fonts following his sketches. Later on, when some variant fonts for use in extended text-setting were requested, I made these in line with the other fonts.
Jeanne de Bont had switched jobs, going to work for Philips Design in Eindhoven. They were facing the problems of producing reasonable screen fonts. They asked me to design a small set of them, and this later grew into the Philips screen font family – something they still use.

‖ **1995** Apparently the Philips people liked working with me, and I got involved in the redesign of the Philishave logo. This was initiated by Dingeman Kuilman, who was head of graphic design at Philips. It was a long process, but one that came to a successful conclusion. Dingeman understood what I could do and started to use my skills, passing on to me the requests he got for all kinds of logos for Philips consumer products. But it was an insight which seemed to die as soon as he left the company – in 1997.
Dingeman persuaded me to come and work full-time for Philips. Since they had enough problems to be solved, this seemed interesting. But the decision proved to be a mistake, and after three months I decided to leave the company. It was too big – the different departments did not know what the others were doing – and they were not willing to understand what on-screen information would mean for them and their products. So, after this little adventure, Philips and I went back to the way we had been used to working with each other – I became freelance again.

‖ **1996** Josée Langen, Peter Paul Kloosterman and I wanted to go on with our design practice Quadraat. I knew that Erik Vos had left the Anton Beeke studio in Amsterdam, and I asked him if he was interested in joining us. After much discussion Peter Paul decided work on his own. We called the new practice Het Lab (The Lab).
The ATypI meeting this year was held in The Hague. We finished *Counterpunch* just in time for it, and presented it there with a panel discussion of type designers.
Philips Kitchen Appliances asked if I could design a script-like typeface

Cellesse

Coiffure dryer

Natura

Profile

for them, with an uncomplicated and up-to-date look, which could be used for the lettering on a certain line of kitchen machinery.
In this year also I gave up teaching in Arnhem and started to teach at Sint Joost Academy in Breda.

|| **1997** Erik and Josée were using Quadraat a good deal. Meanwhile I had expanded it with a bold italic and all the matching small cap fonts. Although Quadraat could be used with other sanserifs, they and others asked me, more and more strongly, to add a matching sanserif. I did this, realizing that really humane sanserif typefaces were available, but still few in number. In the end it became an interesting design problem. A sans without a condensed version is, of course, not really complete. So after a few years I added the condensed variants.
The ATypI meeting was held in Reading this year. I gave a lecture there about the big wooden punches cut by Hendrik van den Keere.
I had also become a visiting teacher at the course in type design and typography at the Royal Academy of Art in The Hague. As well as that, I gave lectures here and there, especially abroad. At the same time customers wanted me to come to briefings. All this got me into the train often, and sometimes I was hardly there at the office. It was clear that my activities were drifting further and further away from daily life in a design studio. So I decided to leave Het Lab. I set up my own business called 'Fred Smeijers plus, tailored type and typography'.

|| **1998** I was invited by the Type Directors Club in New York to join the jury of their annual type design contest and give a lecture about my work. The Bay Area printer Alastair Johnston was also a member of this jury, so we re-met there. He invited me to do an interview by email for his magazine *Ampersand*, which we then did. After New York I travelled to Los Angeles and met up with John Downer, who had invited me to visit a workshop at the annual meeting of a signwriters' association.
I wanted to do this especially because I had started to look into the work of people who made and used letterforms completely outside the printing industry.
Among other things, this led to a small article called 'Commercial lettering versus typography', which was published the following year in the British magazine *Typographic*.
Just around the corner from where I lived in Arnhem, Wigger Bierma

Material from the stencil project with Eric Kindel.

and Karel Martens had started their postgraduate 'workshop' in graphic design and typography – the Werkplaats Typografie. One of the projects we did together was the redesign of the daily bulletin of the Dutch government, the *Staatscourant*, for which I designed a typeface. We gave it the name Arnhem.

FontShop Benelux, Jan Willem Stas and Rick Vermeulen organized a big event in Rotterdam called 'THype'. Together with Evert Bloemsma, I gave the opening lecture. Leading up to this, Jan Middendorp interviewed me for *Items* magazine. This article included the first showing of Fresco, a new typeface of mine.

I travelled to Weimar a couple times in this year, to give workshops on 'The principles of type design' at the Bauhaus University there.

|| **1999** It was a normal year with the usual work. An article I had written on Renard as 'an idiosyncratic revival' appeared in English in the Dutch bibliographic journal *Quaerendo*. I managed to spend some more time on new type designs, including Fresco. Philips Design felt the need for a more humane sanserif as companion to the already existing Philips screen font family, and that took up quite some time.

In this year and the following I focused more on research and writing and tried cut down on public appearances. For this reason of saving time and energy I stopped teaching at Breda.

Onno Bevoort began an internship with me. Then after finishing as a student he returned, working as my assistant to October 2002. He was a great help.

|| **2000** Philips Design put on an exhibition of my work, together with a selection showing the whole range of their work. This was held at their offices in Eindhoven.

I had had a plan to bring young Dutch type designers together under their own label, and had given some time and energy to this. But around this time I gave the plan up, and began to think of other ways of starting a new label under which to publish and distribute fonts.

In this year I started on the design of Sansa. It was intended for personal use, but two years later it would be released within OurType. I designed a sanserif for Canon Europe for use in their manuals, and equipped with enough display variations for the firm's packaging.

At the request of Philips Design I got involved with the development of the typographic material for their new generation of DVD interfaces.

|| **2001** A surprise had come in December 2000. I had been awarded the Gerrit Noordzij Prize – the first person to be given it after Gerrit himself in 1996. In February the prize was handed to me by Gerrit at the Royal Academy of Art in The Hague; Robin Kinross delivered the 'laudatio'.
Another surprise was a request from Eric Kindel at the University of Reading, in England, to participate in a project to reconstruct early stencil letters, and the apparatus that had been used for stencilling. It was a nice chance to investigate the – for me – intriguing topic of stencilled books.
Later in the year the Plantijn Genootschap asked me to give a lecture on the role of the Plantin-Moretus Museum in my research on punchcutting.
Wim Westerveld, together the publisher Zoo and the printers Veenman, organized a collective book called *Letters*. The book included some passages from *Counterpunch*, now translated into Dutch. I gave a lecture at the launch in Amsterdam.

|| **2002** The Arnhem city museum organized an exhibition devoted to local talents – called 'Made in Arnhem' – and of course type design was one of the disciplines exhibited. I was still living in Arnhem then, so took part with three other Arnhem type designers: Martin Majoor, Evert Bloemsma, and Alex Scholing.
Meanwhile the work on the stencil letter project led to a joint lecture with Eric Kindel at the ATypI meeting in Rome.
At the request of Wigger Bierma and Ingo Offermanns, I made a small roman family that breathed a seventeenth-century atmosphere – Custodia.
Erik Vos, of Het Lab, and I made a proposal for lettering on the glass roof of the new Amsterdam central bus station.
For some time Rudy Geeraerts, of FontShop Benelux, and I had shared thoughts and ideas about starting our own font label. Now we decided to get on with it, and in December of this year we published the first announcement of OurType in FS Benelux's *Druk* magazine.

|| **2003** Much of my time this year was taken up by OurType. The label issued printed specimens for the first three types to be issued: Arnhem, Sansa and Fresco.
In addition to this work, I wrote an article on 'The Nature of type design' for the Argentinian magazine *Tipográfica*, and participated in a seminar on stencil letters, organized by Eric Kindel, at the University of Reading.
Another demanding project was the Gerrit Noordzij Prize: this book, the exhibition at the Hague Academy, and the trophy to be given to the next award winner — Erik Spiekermann.

Acknowledgements

Together with my publisher I thank the Royal Academy of Art, The Hague, for its support of the production of this book, made as part of the award of the Gerrit Noordzij Prize in 2001. In particular we thank Anno Fekkes, head of the Department of Graphic Design, for his commitment to this prize.

Special thanks to the firms that commissioned work shown here, especially: Océ-Technologies bv, Venlo; Philips Design, Eindhoven; Canon Europe, Amsterdam; BrandNew Design, Weesp, TBWA\Designers Company, Amstelveen; VBAT, Schiphol.

And special to colleagues who gave suggestions or commissions and then helped to bring the work into existence: Jeanne de Bont, Henk Lamers, Martin Majoor, Wim Westerveld, Jelle Bosma, Dingeman Kuilman, Andrea Fuchs, Erik Vos and José Langen at Het Lab, Peter Matthias Noordzij, Wigger Bierma and Karel Martens at the Werkplaats Typografie, Rudy Geeraerts at FontShop Benelux, Jan Middendorp, Onno Bevoort, and Eric Kindel.

The Plantin-Moretus Museum, Antwerp, has provided long-term stimulation and generous help.

Portions of the text in preparation were read by Erik van Blokland, Teus de Jong, Henk Pel, Just van Rossum, and Bruno Steinert. Thanks to them for helpful critical comments. Thanks to Roland Reuß for lending his copy of *Calligraphy and printing in the sixteenth century*, used in the Typefaces section. Parts of the chapter 'Fifteen years of democratic type?' were first published in *Tipográfica*, no. 54, 2002-2003, in an article titled 'The nature of type design'. Thanks to the editors of the magazine for their initiative in suggesting this article.

Finally, for their patience and trust I am especially grateful to Robin Kinross, Françoise Berserik, Jan Willem Stas, Corina Cotorobai, and Ingo Offermanns.

FS